CYBERSECURITY & THE COURTHOUSE: SAFEGUARDING THE JUDICIAL PROCESS

HON. LEO M. GORDON
DANIEL B. GARRIE

AF690296

Wolters Kluwer

This publication is designed to provide accurate and authoritative information in regard to the subject matter covered. It is sold with the understanding that the publisher and the author(s) are not engaged in rendering legal, accounting, or other professional services. If legal advice or other professional assistance is required, the services of a competent professional should be sought.

—From a *Declaration of Principles* jointly adopted by
a Committee of the American Bar Association and
a Committee of Publishers and Associations

Copyright © 2020 CCH Incorporated. All Rights Reserved.

No part of this publication may be reproduced or transmitted in any form or by any means, including electronic, mechanical, photocopying, recording, or utilized by any information storage or retrieval system, without written permission from the publisher. For information about permissions or to request permissions online, visit us at *www.WoltersKluwerLR.com/policies/permissions-reprints-and-licensing*, or email us at *LRUSpermissions@wolterskluwer.com.*

Published by Wolters Kluwer in New York.

Wolters Kluwer Legal & Regulatory U.S. serves customers worldwide with CCH, Aspen Publishers and Kluwer Law International products.

1 2 3 4 5 6 7 8 9 0

ISBN: 978-1-5438-0975-6

About Wolters Kluwer Legal & Regulatory U.S.

Wolters Kluwer Legal & Regulatory U.S. delivers expert content and solutions in the areas of law, corporate compliance, health compliance, reimbursement, and legal education. Its practical solutions help customers successfully navigate the demands of a changing environment to drive their daily activities, enhance decision quality and inspire confident outcomes.

Serving customers worldwide, its legal and regulatory portfolio includes products under the Aspen Publishers, CCH Incorporated, Kluwer Law International, ftwilliam.com and MediRegs names. They are regarded as exceptional and trusted resources for general legal and practice-specific knowledge, compliance and risk management, dynamic workflow solutions, and expert commentary.

WOLTERS KLUWER SUPPLEMENT NOTICE

This product is updated on a periodic basis with supplements and/or new editions to reflect important changes in the subject matter.

If you would like information about enrolling this product in the update service, or wish to receive updates billed separately with a 30-day examination review, please contact our Customer Service Department at 1-800-234-1660 or email us at: *customer.service@wolterskluwer.com*. You can also contact us at:

Wolters Kluwer
Distribution Center
7201 McKinney Circle
Frederick, MD 21704

Important Contact Information

- To order any title, go to *www.WoltersKluwerLR.com* or call 1-800-638-8437.
- To reinstate your manual update service, call 1-800-638-8437.
- To contact Customer Service, e-mail *customer.service@wolterskluwer.com*, call 1-800-234-1660, fax 1-800-901-9075, or mail correspondence to: Order Department—Wolters Kluwer, PO Box 990, Frederick, MD 21705.
- To review your account history or pay an invoice online, visit *www.WoltersKluwerLR.com/payinvoices.*

Wolters Kluwer

To my wife, Marci, and my children, Sarah and Derek, and Jen, Ben, and Wyattt, for their support, encouragement, and love, which make all things possible

To my wife Sarah, and my children Ella and Leon, for their support, encouragement, and love that allows me to be successful. As my children frequently remind me all the time that they and mom help me make everything go Boomshackalaka

TABLE OF CONTENTS

About the Authors

Foreword

Acknowledgements

Chapter 1 Overview of Cybersecurity and the Courts

Daniel Garrie, Esq. and Judge Leo M. Gordon

§ 1.01 Introduction: Court Vulnerability to Cyber Breaches
§ 1.02 Conclusion

Chapter 2 Essential Commandments of Cybersecurity

Daniel Garrie, Esq., Judge Leo M. Gordon, and Tim Murphy

§ 2.01 Introduction
§ 2.02 Develop and Practice Strong Cyber Hygiene
§ 2.03 Know and Secure Vendors' Networks
§ 2.04 Identify and Protect the "Crown Jewels"
§ 2.05 Practice Your Incident Response Plan
§ 2.06 Create and Develop a Global Communications and Messaging Framework
§ 2.07 Test the Incident Response Plan and Update It Regularly
§ 2.08 Develop a Robust Cyber Threat Monitoring and Sharing Team
§ 2.09 Engage Privacy and Cybersecurity Expertise
§ 2.10 Maintain Government Relationships

Chapter 3 A Survey of Cyber Threats and Their Context

Daniel Garrie, Esq., Judge Leo M. Gordon, David Lawrence, Tim Murphy, and Harvey Rishikof

§ 3.01 Introduction
§ 3.02 The State of Our Digital Union: Necessary Context for Adopting a Risk-Based Approach
§ 3.03 The Threats Landscape for Courts and Court Systems

§ 3.04 The Range of Specific Threats
§ 3.05 Conclusion

Chapter 4 What It Takes to Frustrate the Hacker Knocking at Your Door

Daniel Garrie, Esq., Judge Leo M. Gordon, Greg Kelley, Richard Rushing, and Bill Spernow

§ 4.01 Do not Be the Low-Hanging Fruit
§ 4.02 Proper Password Management Is Essential to Security
§ 4.03 Firewalls: Regulating Who and What Can Access Your System
§ 4.04 Applying Patches: Keeping Your Software as Secure and Up-to-Date as Possible
§ 4.05 Perimeter Security Controls: What It Takes to Keep the Bad Guys Out
§ 4.06 Encryption
§ 4.07 Summary

Chapter 5 Cryptography

Daniel Garrie, Esq., Judge Leo M. Gordon, Rick Borden, and Jeff Stapleton

§ 5.01 Introduction
§ 5.02 Encryption
§ 5.03 Message Authentication
§ 5.04 Digital Signatures
§ 5.05 Key Management
§ 5.06 Other Crypto Considerations
§ 5.07 Conclusion
Appendix 5-1 Chapter Glossary

Chapter 6 ISO Standards

Daniel Garrie, Esq. and Judge Leo M. Gordon

§ 6.01 Introduction
§ 6.02 ISO Standard 27001
§ 6.03 ISO Scope and Certification
§ 6.04 Conclusion

Chapter 7 Defending Against Threats Through Information Sharing

Daniel Garrie, Esq., Judge Leo M. Gordon, Diana Burley, Cindy Donaldson, and Bill Nelson

§ 7.01 Legal Services: A Big Target for Hackers
§ 7.02 Attacks Are Getting More Frequent and More Sophisticated

§ 7.03 There Is Hope: Courts and Court Systems Should Prepare and Share
§ 7.04 The Legal Services Information Sharing and Analysis Organization

Chapter 8 How Courts Can Use the Cybersecurity Framework for Critical Infrastructure

Daniel Garrie, Esq. and Judge Leo M. Gordon

§ 8.01 Introduction
§ 8.02 Overview of the NIST Framework
§ 8.03 The Framework Core: Functions of a Successful Cybersecurity Program
§ 8.04 Assessing Cybersecurity Risk Management Practices Using the Framework Implementation Tiers

Chapter 9 Structure Your Court to Make It Hacker-Proof

Daniel Garrie, Esq., Judge Leo M. Gordon, Greg Kelley, and Bill Spernow

§ 9.01 Internal Network Controls
§ 9.02 Threat Management Versus Risk Management
§ 9.03 Staff—Finding the Right People and Services
§ 9.04 Summary

Index

ABOUT THE AUTHORS

Judge Leo M. Gordon was appointed to the U.S. Court of International Trade in March 2006. Judge Gordon's career is one that is dedicated to public service and began over three decades ago as Assistant Counsel to the Subcommittee on Monopolies and Commercial Law, Committee on the Judiciary, and U.S. House of Representatives. In that capacity, Judge Gordon was the principal attorney responsible for the Customs Courts Act of 1980 that created the U.S. Court of International Trade. For 25 years, Judge Gordon was on the staff at the court, serving first as Assistant Clerk and then as Clerk of the Court until his appointment to the bench. Judge Gordon graduated Phi Beta Kappa from the University of North Carolina at Chapel Hill, and received a J.D. from Emory University School of Law.

Daniel B. Garrie is the founder and managing partner at Law & Forensics. Mr. Garrie is paving the way when it comes to 2018's most pressing cyber security, forensic, and legal issues. He is one of the most sought-after computer forensic expert and special master, cyber mediator, and forensic neutral with Judicial Arbitration and Mediation Services, Inc. (JAMS).

Judges and attorneys laud his reports for their clarity, focus, and ability to help parties settle even the most complex disputes. Mr. Garrie has garnered a national reputation for his experience at the intersection of technology and the law and is as comfortable talking with entrepreneurs, information technology professionals, and developers as he is with lawyers and judges.

In addition to his Law Degree, he holds a Bachelor's and Master's in computer science and appears as comfortable talking with entrepreneurs as he is with developers, lawyers, and judges.

FOREWORD

Having read Judge Leo M. Gordon and Daniel B. Garrie's magnificent work on *Cybersecurity & The Courthouse: Federal, State, and Local*, I shudder now at how naïve and incomplete was the federal judiciary's cyber security framework when I joined the Information Technology Committee of the Judicial Conference of the United States in October 2001. Administration of the federal courts' national network was decentralized, with three internet "gateways," one maintained in Washington, D.C. by the Administrative Office of the U.S. Courts; a second in New Orleans and administered by the United States Court of Appeals for the Fifth Circuit; and the third in San Francisco, administered by the United States Court of Appeals for the Ninth Circuit. Intrusion detection systems protecting the national network from outside attacks were maintained at each gateway. When a dispute over Administrative Office monitoring of internet activity of judiciary staff erupted, the Judges of the Ninth Circuit authorized the de-activation of the intrusion detection system in San Francisco. A large swath of the federal judiciary's network west of the Mississippi and north of Texas was left unprotected from cyberattacks. The dispute between the Administrative Office and the Judges spilled over to the press, with the *New York Times*, *Wall Street Journal*, and *L.A. Times* all writing articles on the brouhaha. Ultimately, a compromise was brokered, the intrusion detection system was re-activated, the IT Committee commissioned the National Security Agency to conduct a network security assessment, and the IT Committee sent a report on network security and privacy to the Judicial Conference in September 2005. By then, I was Chair of the IT Committee, having been appointed to that position by the late Chief Justice William Rehnquist. As Chair, I wish I had available to me Judge Gordon's and Mr. Garrie's book on cybersecurity.

The cybersecurity threats have exploded since my time on the Judicial Conference IT Committee. According to the Verizon 2015 Data Breach Investigations Report, it was not until 2014 that "the term 'data breach' [became] part of the broader public vernacular with *The New York Times* devoting more than 700 articles related to data breaches, versus fewer than 125 the previous year."[1] Given the nature of the problem, Judge Gordon and Mr. Garrie are right to say that the balkanized approach to cybersecurity that was typical in the decentralized court system of the early 2000s cannot work. Instead, a comprehensive and integrated strategy is essential. Indeed, as Judge Gordon and Mr. Garrie point out, the federal judiciary now makes cybersecurity its number one administrative priority.

Judge Gordon and Mr. Garrie have assembled a comprehensive treatise to deal with the ever-mounting threats to the confidentiality, integrity, and availability of judicial records. Judge Gordon and Mr. Garrie describe why the courts, state and federal, are such high value targets. They identify the myriad ways by which the courts' IT systems are targeted, setting out in easy to understand language such arcane matters as the difference between a computer virus and a computer worm. They catalogue the significant risks courts face, from the inadvertent loss of data through staff neglect, to the staff member duped to disclose a password through social engineering, to the weaknesses in cybersecurity posed by the growing "Internet of Things" phenomenon, and to the state-sponsored malicious hackers exploiting an unknown vulnerability in network security. The importance of effective password management is drilled home. They explain how encryption works and why it is critical to encrypt sensitive data, as well as the difference between encryption (data confidentiality) and cryptography (data integrity, authentication, and non-repudiation). Also addressed in great detail are the cybersecurity standards adopted by the International Organization for Standardization (ISO) and the National Institute of Standards and Technology (NIST), with the authors pointing out how courts of any size can use the applicable standards to put into place an effective cybersecurity framework. The importance of cybersecurity information sharing organizations, such as the Legal Services Information Sharing and Analysis Organization, is reported, evoking the possibility of a judiciary information sharing and analysis organization, comprised of state and federal judiciary representatives. And the text concludes with a sound structure to protect court IT systems.

The justice system in the United States has become dependent upon efficient and available IT resources. Valuable data bearing on trade secrets, intellectual property, and national security, to mention just a few, reside on judiciary systems. Judges, their clerks, court staff, the media, and the public rely upon the accessibility and integrity of court records. It is not a stretch to say the rule of law is at stake when it comes to the security of judiciary IT systems. Judge Gordon and

---

[1] 2015 Verizon Data Breaches Investigations Report, p. 1, available at https://enterprise.verizon.com/resources/reports/2015/data-breach-investigation-report_2015.pdf.

Mr. Garrie have assembled a text that is a must read for those charged with protecting the rule of law – judges, court administrators, IT professionals, the legal academy, the press, and the interested general public.

United States Circuit Judge Thomas I. Vanaskie (ret.)
Dunmore, PA
July 29, 2019

ACKNOWLEDGEMENTS

This book is the culmination of a collaborative effort by the co-authors and many people who provided guidance, assistance, and input along the way. We are grateful to the contributing authors for their knowledge and insights, which enabled the co-authors to provide meaningful information to our readers. We also thank those who skillfully assisted us with research, proofreading, and cite checking. We also want to thank Jackie Mazariego, who helped keep the trains running. Lastly, Leo and Daniel want to specially acknowledge John A. Foulks, who served as our substantive editor and aided us in creating the final manuscript. He has our eternal gratitude for his expertise and fine pen.

CHAPTER 1

OVERVIEW OF CYBERSECURITY AND THE COURTS

Daniel Garrie, Esq. and Judge Leo M. Gordon

§ 1.01 Introduction: Court Vulnerability to Cyber Breaches

§ 1.02 Conclusion

> Effective cybersecurity requires any organization—whether a private sector company, a non-profit, or an agency at the state, local, or Federal level—to identify, prioritize, and manage cyber risks across its enterprise. These cyber risks can manifest themselves in many ways, including the increasingly sophisticated techniques that threat actors use to compromise systems, the operation of outdated and unsupported IT, or the malicious links and email attachments that can infect unsuspecting users' machines with malware. The recent government-wide cybersecurity risk assessment process conducted by OMB, in coordination with the DHS, confirms the need to take bold approaches to improve Federal cybersecurity.[1]

Federal Cybersecurity Risk Determination Report and Action Plan, May, 2018.

§ 1.01 INTRODUCTION: COURT VULNERABILITY TO CYBER BREACHES

No one is immune from a cybersecurity incident. Every sector of society—including the courts—is a target for hackers and cyber criminals. The Oxford Dictionaries' English dictionary defines cybersecurity as "the state of being protected against the criminal or unauthorized use of electronic data, or the measures taken to achieve this." All levels of courts throughout the United States—whether federal, state, or local—are deeply affected by this issue.

Courts thus face intense pressure to improve their cybersecurity. With the new use of technology by courts and the legal community, from electronically filing court documents to video conferencing in the courtrooms, the threat of hacking into court systems is real. This book explores the issues surrounding cybersecurity for courts and court systems.

> The landscape of court technology has changed rapidly, as digital tools help facilitate the business process of the court. This proliferation of technology has improved the judiciary's access and transparency, while also significantly increasing data storage and the digital footprint. Consequently, there are multiple entry points for data breaches in the judicial branch. These include judiciary case management systems, networks, servers, cloud storage, software programs, WiFi systems, employee devices, and an array of court-specific technology. . . . [I]nformation is shielded from public view to protect the privacy of litigants, children, witnesses, judges, and employees. Courts are entrusted with these records, and . . . [m]any different stakeholders are negatively impacted—litigants, witnesses, victims, judges, lawyers, court staff, the organization itself, and the public as a whole.[2]

The Federal Judiciary identifies cybersecurity as its top administrative priority. "As Judge Julia Gibbons, chair of the United States Judicial Conference's budget [committee], states, 'Judiciary systems have and will continue to be targeted, like government and

---

[1] Executive Office of the President of the United States: Federal Cybersecurity Risk Determination Report and Action Plan (2018).

[2] Brian McLaughlin, *Cybersecurity: Protecting Court Data Assets 2018,* https://www.ncsc.org/~/media/Microsites/Files/Trends%202018/Cybersecurity-Protecting-Court-Data-Assets.ashx (last visited May 17, 2019).

commercial entities everywhere.' A multitude of entry points exist for cyberattacks or cyber breaches on the judicial branch, including information systems, networks (including WiFi), employee personal devices (including smartphones) and an array of court technology. Beyond the damaging consequences of disrupting court operations, hackers target the trove of sealed information in judiciary systems. A sampling of this data includes:

- "Personal identifiers—including social security numbers, credit cards, and bank accounts.
- Confidential informant names and search warrants in criminal cases.
- Records on cases involving children and families, including adoptions.
- Trade secrets in civil cases involving businesses and corporations.
- Victim data in domestic violence and sexual assault cases.
- Grade jury records and testimony.
- Medical and psychological reports."[3]

The Federal Bureau of Investigation (FBI) defines a cyber incident as 'a past, ongoing, or threatened intrusion, disruption, or other event that impairs or is likely to impair the confidentiality, integrity, or availability of electronic information, information systems, services, or networks.' Four types of cyberattacks are particularly concerning for court officials:

> "**Denial of Service (DoS) attacks**—This type of cyberattack prevents legitimate users from accessing network services. DoS attacks are most commonly effectuated by overwhelming servers with traffic to a specific site.
>
> **Phishing**—This type of attack uses social engineering to solicit personal information from unsuspecting users. Phishing emails appear to look legitimate, but they are not, asking users to enter items such as user names or passwords to compromise accounts.
>
> **Ransomware**—This type of cyberattack infects software and locks access to data until a ransom is paid. Through phishing e-mails, drive-by downloading and unpatched vulnerabilities, hackers attempt to extort users by encrypting their data until the prescribed conditions are met.
>
> **Spyware**—This type of cyberattack, also known as adware, infects a computer by producing pop-up ads, re-directing browsers and monitoring a user's internet activity."[4]

This book is intended to help judges, court executives, and court technology professionals increase their awareness of the issues around cybersecurity and identify possible pathways to address strengths and weaknesses in individual courts and across court systems. Chapter 2 outlines essential commandments of cybersecurity. Chapter 3 focuses on helping courts better understand the language around the various existing types of cyber threats. Chapter 4 addresses what it takes to frustrate the hacker knocking at your door. Chapter 5 defines cryptography and how it relates to the world of cybersecurity. Chapter 6 discusses technology standards of the International Organization for Standardization

[3] Bryan McLaughlin, *Cyber Security: Protecting Court Data, PATIMES* (May 26, 2017), https://patimes.org/cybersecurity-protecting-court-data/.

[4] *Id.*

(ISO) and how they can assist an organization in assessing their vulnerabilities to cyber threats. Chapter 7 deals with the potential of information sharing as a practice that can help defend courts and court systems against cyber threats. Chapter 8 addresses how courts and court systems can effectively use the National Institute of Standards and Technology's (NIST) framework for understanding cybersecurity to improve their critical technology infrastructure. Lastly, chapter 9 identifies steps that courts and court systems can take to reduce their vulnerability to hackers.

§ 1.02 CONCLUSION

Any entity or organization, whether in the public or private sector, is a potential target for hackers and thus a potential victim of a data breach. Courts and court systems are particularly attractive targets for cybercriminals, hacktivists, or other malicious actors due to the sensitive data they hold. The potential consequences for courts or court systems that fall victim to a cyber breach are found on multiple levels. At a minimum, there is a financial cost associated with investigating and mitigating the breach. Beyond these come costs associated with addressing potential ethics and code-of-conduct violations by personnel as well as issues of reputational damage. There comes an overall cost to public confidence in the courts, for they are institutions committed to protecting and promoting the rule of law. Although courts and court systems are beginning to recognize their vulnerability to cyber threats, fiscal and personnel challenges affect the ability of courts and court systems, in varying degrees, to respond to potential threats or take steps to reduce their vulnerabilities. The purpose and goal of this book is to assist courts and court systems in better understanding the nature of cyber threats, and then in formulating adequate protections against those threats.

CHAPTER 2

ESSENTIAL COMMANDMENTS OF CYBERSECURITY

Daniel Garrie, Esq., Judge Leo M. Gordon, and Tim Murphy

§ 2.01 Introduction

§ 2.02 Develop and Practice Strong Cyber Hygiene

§ 2.03 Know and Secure Vendors' Networks

§ 2.04 Identify and Protect the "Crown Jewels"

§ 2.05 Practice Your Incident Response Plan

§ 2.06 Create and Develop a Global Communications and Messaging Framework

§ 2.07 Test the Incident Response Plan and Update It Regularly

§ 2.08 Develop a Robust Cyber Threat Monitoring and Sharing Team

§ 2.09 Engage Privacy and Cybersecurity Expertise

§ 2.10 Maintain Government Relationships

§ 2.01 INTRODUCTION

Imagine that the most sensitive information contained in a court filing or other litigation document in the court's possession is stolen. The court is faced with disclosing this breach to lawyers, litigants, and other interested parties. While the information technology (IT) department, senior managers, and judges are scrambling to figure out what to do, they soon realize all of their court's records are missing, and someone is demanding that the court pay a ransom in exchange for the release of those records. Now, imagine further that the court has no alternative but to pay the demand (in bitcoins) to ensure the security of its own record-keeping system.

One has to look no further than the Panama Papers, the 2018 cyberattack on the City of Atlanta's municipal services, or any of the other noteworthy headlines to realize how quickly and easily our digital platforms can be used against us. Although the Internet has delivered on its promise of global access and efficiency, it also accelerates and scales up the darker forms of human activity—theft, fraud, extortion, blackmail, espionage (state and corporate), terrorism, insider trading, property destruction, and criminal mischief. Soon, the Internet of Things (IoT) will even more seamlessly connect our devices to everything we need—as well as everything we need to fear.

As we are continuing to learn, the Internet was built for connectivity and speed, not for security or protection. For criminals, rogue states, and mischievous actors, the digital world has become a "promised land" of low risk and high reward, offering borderless reach, assured anonymity, and defenseless victims who, under the current state of the law, are largely not permitted to fight back.

Foreign governments, state-sponsored agents, criminals, terrorists, and lone actors are increasingly targeting our data systems and information networks. The finances, trade secrets, and operations of our enterprises as well as the identities and privacy of our citizens are at constant risk. With an eye toward future infiltration and disruption, networks that control critical governmental infrastructure (e.g., power grids, manufacturing plants, communications, health and transportation systems, law enforcement authorities, and courts) are being probed for vulnerabilities. The Federal Government—as well as our leading military and law enforcement agencies—have been repeatedly targeted by cybercriminals. Hackers in China and Russia are targeting U.S. defense contractors. North Korea's alleged cyberattack on Sony Pictures in 2014 destroyed data, disabled thousands of computers, and disrupted the executive suite. Distributed denial-of-service attacks have been launched against governmental agencies, the media, utilities, banks, hospitals, and manufacturing firms, to name just a few.

With more than 100 a hundred million Americans' personal data having been compromised in recent years—including credit card information and medical records—it is no surprise that nine out of ten Americans say they feel they have lost control of their personal information. These cyber threats are among the most urgent risks to America's economic and national security and to the personal safety of its citizens.

As America's cyber adversaries have grown more sophisticated and active—emboldened by their successes and the absence of consequences—the need to be proactive, nimble, and resilient has increased. In this environment, it is easy for even the most sophisticated governmental and non-governmental entities to feel overwhelmed. The Federal Government, which is obligated to protect the information provided to it by the American people, has a unique responsibility to lead. But the fact is, even the U.S. Government does not have all the tools it needs in place, and in many areas, it lacks even the safeguards required of many private-sector entities.

This volume offers a great amount of detail, but the following "commandments" are proven, commonsense, immediately available steps to take for security.

§ 2.02 DEVELOP AND PRACTICE STRONG CYBER HYGIENE

- Conduct full background checks and consider continuous evaluations of employees rather than one-and-done or even periodic background checks of personnel. This mitigates the risk from "insider" threats.
- Implement a robust password policies or another advanced means of multifactor authentication.
- Ensure the security of computing and communication devices, especially when traveling abroad.
- Train employees about email etiquette and "spear-phishing" schemes.
- Keep personnel up-to-date about relevant incidents, causes, and consequences.
- Increase and demonstrate cybersecurity common sense as part of performance reviews.
- Utilize surveillance and malware detection as well as "detonation" software.
- Assess security requirements for encrypted phones, laptops, and smart devices.

§ 2.03 KNOW AND SECURE VENDORS' NETWORKS

- Limit vendors' access to only what they need to perform their respective services.
- Conduct due-diligence investigations into the backgrounds of vendors with access to the court. Enterprise security is only as strong as its weakest link. Consider continuous evaluation of vendors for any changed risks.
- Review existing contract language and understand vendors' cybersecurity protocols.
- Contractually bind vendors to certain security standards and protocols.
- Identify, rank, engage, and audit third-party vendors, paying attention to where they are headquartered and how important they are to court operations. Vendors must be willing to become partners in maintaining your security.
- Require vendors who provide critical data to disclose cyber incidents within seventy-two hours of their occurrence.

§ 2.04 IDENTIFY AND PROTECT THE "CROWN JEWELS"

- Identify, and separately protect, critical data and systems. This might be litigant and other sensitive court data, or intra-court and judiciary-wide communications.
- Verify and update processes with judges and the management team.

- Implement and regularly update appropriate controls, systems, and processes to protect systems.
- Verify, validate, and regularly test security systems to ensure the continued protection of critical data in the most effective manner.
- Introduce encryption of data (including data-at-rest and data-in-transit), for an added layer of protection.

§ 2.05 PRACTICE YOUR INCIDENT RESPONSE PLAN

- Engage the judges and management team in developing a cross-functional incident response plan, and designate a team to carry out the plan in the event of an attack.
- Identify specific contacts from among the leadership of the judiciary, law enforcement, and appropriate executive agencies before there has been a cyberattack.
- Identify appropriate judiciary-wide technical, legal, and public relations experts who should be on-call for the inevitable cyber incident.
- Focus on the range of potential attacks, their motivations, and their objectives (e.g., theft, denial of service, ransom, or publication).
- Identify applicable privacy and non-disclosure laws, and work with judiciary-wide leadership, appropriate executive agencies, and the bar to protect the confidentiality of litigant, lawyer, and court information.

§ 2.06 CREATE AND DEVELOP A GLOBAL COMMUNICATIONS AND MESSAGING FRAMEWORK

- Ensure that any communications plan covers all relevant constituencies—judges, staff, government and private counsel, litigants, and third-party vendors.
- Identify all government entities (Federal, State, municipal, and foreign) that will expect disclosure.
- Identify media, social media, and source channels for disseminating court-related information.
- If necessary, work with judiciary-wide messaging experts to ensure a coordinated response.

§ 2.07 TEST THE INCIDENT RESPONSE PLAN AND UPDATE IT REGULARLY

- Utilize independent resources to conduct annual penetration testing to identify weaknesses in IT networks, infrastructure, and employee practices.
- Report the results to the court's executive management team on a regular basis.
- Modify the response plan to reflect the results of testing.

§ 2.08 DEVELOP A ROBUST CYBER THREAT MONITORING AND SHARING TEAM

- Monitor cyber threats both internally and externally, and regularly probe IT systems for weaknesses.
- Monitor the Internet, social media, and the Dark Web for stolen data and information on judges, key management staff, and court operations.
- Test employee practices and compliance with security procedures.
- Participate in government cyber threat sharing platforms, and ensure your organization is able to act on the intelligence provided.

§ 2.09 ENGAGE PRIVACY AND CYBERSECURITY EXPERTISE

- Maintain contacts with whom to share information and threat intelligence, including about best practices and solutions.
- Seek advice from other governmental entities as sources of valuable information and assistance.
- Maintain and update information obtained from these sources on a regular basis.
- Consult judiciary-wide counsel to ensure that any chosen cybersecurity solutions are compatible with applicable laws.

§ 2.10 MAINTAIN GOVERNMENT RELATIONSHIPS

- Identify and build relationships with key judiciary-wide personnel and agencies in the court's jurisdiction. They can be critical partners in both prevention and response, and can be sought out for advice, needed information, and assistance. Their expertise and intelligence can be invaluable.
- Seek advice on privacy-related legal issues to ensure that cybersecurity solutions comply with applicable statutes and regulations.
- Maintain and update key contacts and related information on a regular basis.
- Be clear that the time to forge these relationships is before hand, rather than after there has been a cybersecurity breach.

CHAPTER 3

A SURVEY OF CYBER THREATS AND THEIR CONTEXT

Daniel Garrie, Esq., Judge Leo M. Gordon, David Lawrence, Tim Murphy, and Harvey Rishikof

§ 3.01 Introduction

§ 3.02 The State of Our Digital Union: Necessary Context for Adopting a Risk-Based Approach

§ 3.03 The Threats Landscape for Courts and Court Systems

§ 3.04 The Range of Specific Threats

[A] Theft or Loss of a Device
[B] Employee Criminality: The Insider Threat
[C] Social Engineering
[D] Insider or Privilege—Abuse Hostilities
[E] Bypassing of Security Controls
[F] Network Port Probes
[G] Unpatched Software Vulnerabilities
[H] Denial-of-Service Attacks
[I] Group Phishing
[J] Spear Phishing
[K] Website Exploits and Browser Security
[L] Bots and Command & Control Centers
[M] Viruses and Worms
[N] Trojan Horses
[O] Zero-Day Exploits
[P] Spyware

§ 3.05 Conclusion

§ 3.01 INTRODUCTION

This chapter serves as an introduction to the range of cyberattacks that many court systems may confront. As part of this process, we outline the rationale for why a court's digital communications and other records constitute high-value targets to a wide range of diversely motivated actors, many of whom are armed with increasingly sophisticated technologies (as well as proven low-tech methods) for penetrating court systems. In doing so, we seek to provide context for continued thinking about and weighing of a risk-based approach to court security and data protection protocols.

At the outset, it is critical that courts and court systems recognize the breadth and depth of cyber attackers' methods, their long-term incentives for targeting court systems,[1] and the range of consequences of a successful attack. Principally, cyber attackers will have at least one of three objectives: (1) to gain administrator or specific-user access to a court's computer systems; (2) to cause physical or virtual damage to a court's computer or data storage systems; and (3) to potentially delegitimize individual judges, the judicial system, or both together.

The first goal, gaining access, allows cybercriminals to view court data and communications, and would generally enable a sufficiently sophisticated actor to transfer, alter, or delete this information, often without detection.[2] The second goal, causing physical or virtual damage to a court's systems, constitutes a malicious and destructive act upon the enterprise.[3] It generally requires no special access, because the attacks are either external or "insider"-driven (e.g., a denial-of-service attack), or are exploitative (e.g., attacking an unpatched operating system). Significantly, both forms of attacks can be deployed to steal confidential or market-sensitive information as well as to hold data and systems hostage

---

[1] American Bar AssociationCybersecurity Legal Task Force Section of Science & Technology Law, *Report to the House of Delegates: Resolution 109* (Aug. 2014) http://www.americanbar.org/content/dam/aba/administrative/house_of_delegates/resolutions/2014_hod_annual_meeting_109.authcheckdam.pdf. ("The threat of cyber attacks against law firms is growing. Lawyers and law offices are facing unprecedented challenges from the widespread use of electronic records and mobile devices. There are many reasons for hackers to target the information being held by law firms. They collect and store large amounts of critical, highly valuable corporate records, including intellectual property, strategic business data, and litigation-related theories and records collected through e-discovery.").

[2] Raymond R. Panko, Business Data Networks and Telecommunications (4th ed. 2003) ("The hacker is now in a position to wreak havoc in the system by means such as reading or altering sensitive information, changing or deleting key files, wiping out the hard drive, and using the compromised target to launch attacks against other targets."). While this access can be actively used to cause harm to a court, it is also possible to use that access to passively ingest a court's or a litigant's sensitive data. Imagine a court that has a robust intellectual property docket. If a cyber criminal wanted to engage in corporate espionage, it is unlikely it would be able to access a company's research; but once that information is sent to a court in the context of an intellectual property litigation, it might be in significant jeopardy if the court does not have proper cybersecurity processes in place.

[3] Al Bento & Regina Bento, *Empirical Test of a Hacking Model: An Exploratory Study*, 14 Comm. Ass'n for Info. Sys. 678, 68 (2004). ("When hackers are unable to achieve control of the target, they often express their frustration by launching Denial-of-Service (DoS) attacks (such as *Smurf*, *Fraggle* and *Syn*) that disrupt services or make them inaccessible to legitimate users, networks, and systems.").

as part of an extortion scheme that requires payment of a ransom (ransomware).[4] The third objective, delegitimizing, would involve putting individual judges' communications out on the Internet, either to embarrass them or the judiciary or to discredit their impartiality or neutrality.[5]

Cyberattacks can be launched either directly against a court's systems or by exploiting employees, litigants, lawyers, vendors, and suppliers (e.g., its software providers); or they can come through its data storage, human resource (HR) materials, and electronic filings.[6] In sum, law courts and court systems must understand that they are neither immune nor unique among other kinds of enterprises in the following regard: Their security chains will be only as strong as their weakest internal and external links.

As targets, however, courts do have a special allure for cybercriminals. Inherently, they will always be high-value targets because they have special information that is core to the relationship between litigants and their counsel. This includes sensitive confidential communications, trade secrets, financial data, and intellectual property (IP) as well as market-sensitive information about litigation, government investigations, mergers and acquisitions, and criminal proceedings.

Irrespective of the nature and purpose of the attack, courts must anticipate the wide-ranging potential harms to and contagions of commercial, legal, financial, and reputational matters that come from being "hacked." By its very nature, the damage from an attack can be highly consequential and long term, affecting lawyer-client relationships, day-to-day operations, and hard- and soft-dollar costs as well as internal and public confidence in the legal system and in the rule of law.

Inevitably, a breach will also implicate difficult cost-benefit (and hindsight) analyses of the need for enhanced security, disclosure to litigants and lawyers, government cooperation, media response, remediation, and enterprise resiliency. A successful attack on a court or court system draws quick and repeated inquiries from litigants, lawyers, government entities, and the media. Attacks on courts and court systems are of great interest to these constituencies (as well as to the public at large), not only because of the highly sensitive nature of attorney-client matters—and the often embarrassing secrets revealed—but also because many courts and court systems have developed extensive "best" practices in advising litigants and lawyers on the very issues of cybersecurity, data privacy, information protection, crisis management, and contingency planning. This is an irony that has not been lost on the diverse community of hackers that seek to target courts.

The nature, timing, coordination, and messaging of a court's or a court system's response to a breach is therefore critical. Prior planning and preparation will always be essential.

---

[4] Jason Proctor, *Ransomware Hackers Pose Threat to B.C. Law Firms*, CBC News (Jan. 12, 2015), http://www.cbc.ca/beta/news/canada/british-columbia/ransomware-hackers-pose-threat-to-b-c-law-firms-1.2898490.

[5] *See* Suzanne Spaulding & Harvey Rishikof, *How Putin Works to Weaken Faiht in the Rule of Law and Our Justice System*, Lawfare (Sept. 17, 2018).

[6] *See* Phil Huggins, *Supplier Security,* Managing Partner 17 (Mar. 20, 2015).

§ 3.02 THE STATE OF OUR DIGITAL UNION: NECESSARY CONTEXT FOR ADOPTING A RISK-BASED APPROACH

As we now know all too well, the Internet was constructed for universal connectivity and accessibility, and not with an eye toward security or containing the darker sides of human behavior.[7] Although the Internet has delivered on its promise of social and economic progress, it also will continue to deliver unparalleled opportunities to those seeking to scale up global conflict, terrorism, criminal activity, state and industrial espionage, and vandalism. In the near future, the Internet of Things (IoT) will not only accelerate new ways for entities to provide even greater access and efficiencies but will also offer bad actors a scalable means to further compromise enterprise and personal security.[8]

Increasingly, rogue governments, state-sponsored agents, criminals, terrorists, and lone actors are targeting global data systems and information networks. Irrespective of where data is held, the finances, trade secrets, and operations of our enterprises as well as the identities and privacy of our citizens are at constant risk. On a daily basis, denial-of-service and data-theft attacks are launched against governmental agencies, courts, the media, utilities, banks, hospitals, retailers, manufacturers, and professional service firms to name only a few.[9]

Networks that control and support corporate and governmental infrastructures (power grids, manufacturing plants, and communications, health, finance, and transportation systems) are being probed for vulnerabilities with an eye toward future infiltration and disruption.[10] The Federal Government as well as our leading military and law enforcement agencies have been repeatedly targeted by cybercriminals, as for example with the intrusion into the Office of Personnel Management in 2015 during which the personal information of millions of current and former federal employees was stolen.[11] Hackers in China and Russia continue to target leading players in the private sector as well as government agencies.[12] North Korea's alleged cyberattack on Sony Pictures in 2014 destroyed data, disabled thousands of computers, and disrupted the entire executive-suite

---

[7] Shahida Sweeney, *Internet Not Designed for Security, Warns International Expert*, CIO (Mar. 2, 2015), http://www.cio.com.au/article/569270/internet-designed-security-warns-international-expert/.

[8] Robert Plant, *Here's Why the Internet of Things Could Be a Security Nightmare*, Wall Street Journals (Feb. 23, 2016), http://blogs.wsj.com/experts/2016/02/23/heres-why-it-should-be-scared-of-the-internet-of-things/.

[9] Kim Zetter, *The Biggest Security Threats We'll Face in 2016*, WIRED (Jan. 1, 2016), http://www.wired.com/2016/01/the-biggest-security-threats-well-face-in-2016/.

[10] Grant Gross, *Cyberattack Could Knock Out Huge Chunk of U.S. Electric Grid*, Computer World (Apr. 14, 2016), http://www.computerworld.com/article/3056617/security/cyberattack-could-knock-out-huge-chunk-of-us-electric-grid.html.

[11] Kate Vinton, *21.5 Million Americans Were Compromised in OPM's Second Breach*, Forbes, (July 19, 2015), http://www.forbes.com/sites/katevinton/2015/07/09/21-5-million-americans-were-compromised-in-opms-second-breach/?ss=Security&utm_source=twitter&utm_medium=social&utm_content=Oktopost-twitter-profile&utm_campaign=Oktopost-2015-07%20General%20Campaign#302475676916.

[12] Barrie Barber, *Cyber Hackers from China, Russia Target Area Defense Firms*, Dayton Daily News (Mar. 25, 2016), https://www.daytondailynews.com/news/local-military/cyber-hackers-target-area-defense-firms/LQxfnSauwAn29WECoPqdqN/.

layer of that company.[13] In 2016, Iranian operatives were criminally charged with hacking into New York's water systems.[14] On October 21, 2016, a cyberattack against Dynamic Network Services, Inc. (Dyn) denied millions of Internet users access to websites including Twitter, Reddit, and Netflix.[15] With the expansion of the IoT, the number of points of access from which to launch such an attack has increased dramatically, as it includes smart devices, web cameras, appliances, and other non-secure connections to the Internet.[16]

With more than 100 million Americans' personal data compromised in recent years—including credit card, bank, tax, and medical records—it is no surprise that nine out of ten Americans say they feel they have lost control of their personal information.[17] These cyber threats are among the most urgent risks to America's economic and national security, the personal safety of its citizens, and the integrity of governmental records.

The need for enterprises (private and governmental) to be proactive, nimble, and resilient has increased as cyber adversaries, emboldened by their successes and by the absence of consequences, have grown more sophisticated and active. In this environment, even the most sophisticated entities easily feel overwhelmed. No single enterprise or source possesses all the answers.

The Federal Government, which is obligated to protect the information provided to it by the American people, has a unique responsibility to lead. The fact is, though, that even the U.S. Government does not have in place all the tools it needs; and in many areas, it lacks safeguards that local and State governments as well as many businesses require.[18]

Lessons have been learned from both our successes and failures, so it is essential that courts and court systems continue to share hard-earned collective wisdom.[19] For this reason, various sectors including the legal sector have recognized the need to form information-sharing groups to disseminate information about cyber threats and other vulnerabilities.[20] In the future, private entities will be better able to share information with

---

[13] Bob Orr, *Why the U.S. Was Sure North Korea Hacked Sony*, CBS (Jan. 29, 2015), http://www.cbsnews.com/news/why-the-u-s-government-was-sure-north-korea-hacked-sony/; Erik Larson et al., *U.S. to Charge Iran in Cyber Attacks Against Banks, New York Dam—Sources*, Reuters (Mar. 23, 2016), http://www.reuters.com/article/us-usa-iran-cyber-iduskcn0wp2nm.

[14] Dustin Volz & Jim Finkle, *U.S. Indicates Iranian for Hacking Dozens of Banks, New York Dam*, Reuters (Mar. 24, 2016), https://www.reuters.com/article/us-usa-iran-cyber/u-s-indicts-iranians-for-hacking-dozens-of-banks-new-york-dam-idUSKCN0WQ1JF.

[15] Haley Sweetland Edwards, *How Webcams Helped Bring down the Internet,* TIME (Oct. 25, 2016), https://time.com/4542600/internet-outage-web-cams-hackers/

[16] *Cyber Attacks Take Down Major Websites*, Crain's Chicago Business (Oct. 21, 2016), www.chicagobusiness.com/article/20161021/NEWS08/161029970.

[17] Dan Kedmey, *9 in 10 Americans Feel They've Lost Control of Their Personal Data,* TIME (Nov. 12, 2014), http://time.com/3521166/privacy-personal-data-report/.

[18] *U.S. Government "Worse Than All Major Industries" on Cybersecurity*, Reuters (Apr. 15, 2016), http://www.nbcnews.com/tech/tech-news/u-s-government-worse-all-major-industries-cyber-security-n556461.

[19] *See* David Lawrence et al., *"Ten Commandments" of Cyber Security Can Enhance Safety,* Knowledge@Wharton (Feb. 24, 2016), http://knowledge.wharton.upenn.edu/article/how-the-ten-commandments-of-cyber-security-can-enhance-safety/.

[20] The effort is coordinated by the Financial Services Information Sharing and Analysis Center, which oversees the legal group and similar entities that focus on other industries such as retail. The group includes Sullivan & Cromwell, Debevoise & Plimpton, Paul Weiss Rifkind Wharton & Garrison, Allen & Overy, and

each other and to coordinate their efforts through such programs as the newly-created Cybersecurity Information Sharing Act.

The Executive Branch has repeatedly warned of the existential nature of our cyber exposures.[21] To this end, the Federal Government formed the bipartisan Commission on Enhancing National Cybersecurity to focus on long-term solutions in 2016.[22] This Commission, composed of top business, strategic, and technology experts from inside and outside the Government, was to provide specific recommendations for bolstering cybersecurity awareness and protections across the public and private sectors over a ten-year period.[23] This was a significant step toward recognizing and responding to our exposures.

The Commission ended up issuing its final report on December 1, 2016. Fortunately, when it comes to understanding our global state of preparedness and our ability to respond to cyberattacks, there are some consensus views to inform *anyone interested in cybersecurity* about the nature of these exposures:[24]

- The immense security costs now imposed upon public and private enterprises solely to stay in operation represent effectively the single greatest protection cost in modern history.
- Cyber risk is now a systemic threat to national security, economic sustainability, safety, public confidence, the efficacy of our legal system, and the freedoms that constitute our way of life. Cyberattacks have led to the greatest theft and transference of money, information, intellectual property, and state secrets in modern history.
- There are only three types of entities left operating in the world (including courts and law firms): those that have been hacked, those that are going to be hacked, and those that already have been hacked, but don't yet know it.
- The consensus on the annual cost of cyberattacks to the global economy is around 600 billion dollars, but the true, "whisper" amount of financial damage dwarfs this estimate. Many successful intrusions are never detected. Other attacks go unreported due to national security considerations and legal and business concerns over lawyer-client relationships, litigation, and reputational harm.
- The occurrence of a large, catastrophic, and systemic attack is no longer a matter of if but of when and of how costly: to life, property, reputations, the economy,

Linklaters. It will be affiliated with the financial industry's forum for cyber threat discussions, the Financial Services Information Sharing and Analysis Center (FS-ISAC), according to William Nelson, CEO of FS-ISAC. Christine Simmons & Nell Gluckman, *Law Firms to Form Cybersecurity Alliance,* The American Lawyer (Mar. 4, 2015), http://www.americanlawyer.com/id=1202719660496/Law-Firms-to-Form-Cybersecurity-Alliance?slreturn=20160319022150.

[21] Barack Obama, *Protecting U.S. Innovation from Cyberthreats,* Wall St. J. (Feb. 9, 2016), http://www.wsj.com/articles/protecting-u-s-innovation-from-cyberthreats-1455012003.

[22] Roberta Rampton, *Obama Names Cyber Experts from Business, Academia to New Panel,* Reuters (Apr. 13, 2016), http://www.reuters.com/article/us-usa-cyber-obama-idUSKCN0XA2O1.

[23] *Id.*

[24] David Lawrence et al., *We Don't Need a Crisis to Act Unitedly against Cyber Threats,* Knowledge@Wharton (June 1, 2015), *available at* http://knowledge.wharton.upenn.edu/article/we-dont-need-a-crisis-to-act-unitedly-against-cyber-threats/.

the integrity of our legal structure, and our overall sense of confidence and security.

- If you can imagine it, hackers can do it. And even if you cannot imagine it, hackers have been able to—and are working on it.
- Only a small fraction of the threat becomes known to the public through headlines and episodic disclosures. Rest assured: There is no shortage of plans or talent for launching systemic strikes against critical infrastructure—defense, power, transportation, telecom, medical, finance, and court systems.
- Officials fear that it may take a cyber 9/11 event before we wake up and acknowledge the magnitude of this threat. By then, broad-scale and irreparable harm will have occurred, and we may be locked into a zero-sum blame game.
- Cybersecurity is not merely a technology issue in need of a patch. Rather, technology and its portals are the newest means for a widening range of individual, group, and state-sponsored actors to achieve familiar ends. In reality, it is about fraud, theft, state and industrial espionage, extortion, illicit finance, geopolitical conflict, terrorism, economic disruption, human rights violations, vandalism, and erosion of belief in the rule of law. There is no simple fix.
- Most consequential threats emanate from a relatively discrete group of states, state-sponsored actors, and state-protected groups. Long-term solutions will have to reflect geopolitical realities.
- Be they criminals, spies, terrorists, "hacktivists," or enemy states, those behind cyberattacks are rational actors. The infamous 1930s bank robber, Willie Sutton, reportedly offered a simple explanation as to why he robbed banks: "It's where the money is." Whether the hacker is an outsider breaking in or an insider attacking from within, our connected networks offer the keys to the castles that contain, among other assets, our sensitive litigation information (both civil and criminal), our money, state and military secrets, our operational systems, and our IP, business strategies, market-sensitive information, private communications, personal identities, legal advice, and reputations.
- Cybercrime remains a virtually perfect crime as well as an act of war. It is low-risk and high-reward. It is agile, cheap, and remotely scalable. It morphs and innovates in ways that leave enforcement officials fighting yesterday's battles with yesterday's weapons. Victims have little or no recourse. Cybercrime does not fit within our current perspectives on and processes for dealing with domestic or international crime. There are no laws, treaties, or boundaries to limit tactics, weapons, and targeting of civilians. Easily cloaked and launched from safe havens, cybercrime carries little risk of detection, prevention, apprehension, or punishment. With so much to gain and so little to lose, why should cybercriminals stop?
- Cyberattack victims unfairly shoulder the blame. In the Alice-in-Wonderland aftermath of cyberattacks, the perpetrators are often beyond the law while the victimized enterprise stands trial. As defendants, enterprises are convicted of knowing that they were attractive, inviting the assault, and then failing to fend off their attackers.
- Our lack of coordination is inconsistent with democratic models for security. Global security has always required partnerships between government bodies and an

informed and committed citizenry. Unfortunately, even the seemingly simple decision to report an attack to appropriate authorities involves a complex calculus about likely costs and uncertain benefits. Critical issues about confidentiality, privacy, information sharing, and safe-harbor notifications have not yet been sufficiently addressed. The degree to which international accords, such as enforcement and notification protocols, will be in play—particularly the ones involving international commercial litigation—is unknown. An international group of governmental experts convened by a resolution of the United Nations General Assembly failed to achieve any consensus in this area as recently as June, 2017.[25]

- Even the most sophisticated (and costliest) efforts at prevention and detection have proven only partially effective, more useful in delaying the inevitable or deflecting the contagion onto another entity that put up a weaker resistance. Institutions are asking themselves, "How fast and nimble do I have to be to outrun this bear?" In the short term, the answer is perhaps, "Just faster than the other guys." In the longer term, the bear is still out there.
- In cyberspace, supply-chain security matters. As noted earlier, a court's information security chain is only as strong as its weakest link who has access.
- To the degree there is a balkanized approach to cybersecurity, it is likely to fit a popular definition of insanity: We are doing the same thing over and over again (but without even expecting a different result). No single entity, sector, or nation can manage this risk on its own. Robust procedures and protections for shared knowledge and resources must be an essential component of a cybersecurity strategy, particularly for courts and court systems.

§ 3.03 THE THREAT LANDSCAPE FOR COURTS AND COURT SYSTEMS

Unfortunately, the legal disclaimer that attaches to the marketing of mutual funds—*past performance may not be indicative of future returns*—does not apply to our cyber exposures. To the contrary: When it comes to cyberattacks, even if history does not exactly repeat itself, it rhymes close enough.

While the number of hackers and cybercriminals has increased substantially over the last several years,[26] the fundamental approaches they utilize to compromise the integrity of courts and court systems are the same, essentially because the core elements of computer technology have not changed. Because core methodologies have remained unchanged for years, enhanced "hacking tools" have been developed. These easily accessible sets of software have enabled even novice hackers to engage in very sophisticated cyber hostilities.

Thus it is essential for courts and court systems to realize that—even if they believe themselves to be low profile—they will be attractive and susceptible to a wide range of

[25] *United Nations Groups of Governmental Experts*, NUCLEAR THREAT INITIATIVE, https://www.nti.org/learn/treaties-and-regimes/united-nations-groups-governmental-experts/#communications (last visited June 4, 2019).

[26] *The Rise of the Hacker*, THE ECONOMIST (Nov. 5, 2015), https://www.economist.com/business/2015/11/05/the-rise-of-the-hacker.

actors seeking access to their information for a variety of reasons.[27] Because courts are warehouses of sensitive and personally identifiable data, they must recognize that in many ways they are the perfect victims: high-impact, high-vulnerability, silent sufferers.[28]

- Courts are repositories of communications and other sensitive information about litigants and lawyers which, in the wrong hands, can be readily used for inappropriate and illegal gain. This includes information about IP, trade secrets, finances, mergers, acquisitions, commercial strategies, government investigations, criminal proceedings, and indicia of likely litigation outcomes.
- Historically, courts have not been front-line targets for cyberattacks. Accordingly, as a general matter they have not invested as heavily as other enterprises in security resources and personnel. But adversaries have indeed targeted court systems in our country.[29]
- Courts are understandably reluctant to disclose the possibility of a breach, lest they lose the confidence and trust of their lawyers, litigants, and the public.[30]

As a result, the Federal Bureau of Investigation (FBI) and other authorities have issued a series of alerts to warn the legal community about the increasing occurrence of and potential for attacks.[31] Indeed, recent events prove that the warnings from law enforcement officials have been serious. As hacking tools and hackers-for-hire proliferate in certain corners of the Internet, it has become easier for criminals to breach computer networks as a way to further a range of crimes, from insider trading to IP and identity theft to extortion.

In its 2015 Legal Technology Survey, the American Bar Association reported that one in four law firms with at least 100 attorneys has experienced a data breach.[32] The breaches were blamed on hacker penetrations, website attacks, "phishing" schemes, and

[27] For example, parties to matrimonial proceedings may unlawfully access their former spouse's computer or phone. *See* Henry Gornbein, *Divorce, Hacking, and Criminal Prosecution,* Huffington Post (Jan. 12, 2011), https://www.huffpost.com/entry/divorce-hacking-and-crimi_b_805257?guccounter=1&guce_referrer=aHR0cHM6Ly93d3cuZ29vZ2xlLmNvbS8&guce_referrer_sig=AQAAABc3kJ-Li3slrCnJSKeKEqoeb3oReP-0abu8s9RoIayzb0vFYg9WVscdSMHQcMXGygtUhKMq4zQMP0hFFZiTmJ0_ttFj6ydLhf_dbRx1W_tNpPGC7EEPQJXchmZq8BS3A5eNb9BpS_i0CnFM-EqhWVcDPxuda0AX3p416reXqYhg.

[28] Drew T. Simshaw, *Legal Ethics and Data Security: Our Individual and Collective Obligation to Protect Client Data,* 32 Am. J. Trial. Advoc. 549, 550 (2015).

[29] *See* Heather A. Conley, *The Kremlin Playbook*, CSIS (Oct. 13, 2016), https://www.csis.org/analysis/kremlin-playbook

[30] Indeed, one of the hardest questions for law firms is the determination of when they are required to publicly disclose a data breach to a client and regulators. Forty-seven U.S. States have their own breach notification laws, forcing law firms and other companies to navigate a patchwork of different rules. *See* John Clabby & Joseph Swanson, *Developments in Cybersecurity: Privacy Laws, Hacking Beyond Customer Data, and Communicating with Corporate Boards*, JD Supra (Jan. 3, 2016), http://www.jdsupra.com/legalnews/developments-in-cybersecurity-privacy-99147/.

[31] Matthew Goldstein, *Law Firms Are Pressed on Security for Data*, Dealbook (Mar. 26, 2014), http://dealbook.nytimes.com/2014/03/26/law-firms-scrutinized-as-hacking-increases/?_php=true.

[32] Melissa Maleske, *1 in 4 Law Firms Are Victims of a Data Breach*, Law360 (Sept. 22, 2015), http://www.law360.com/articles/705657/1-in-4-law-firms-are-victims-of-a-data-breach.

stolen or lost smartphones or computers.[33] In March, 2016, it was reported that cyber thieves had broken into two of the prominent law firms that represent Fortune 500 companies and Wall Street banks.[34] Presently, U.S. authorities reportedly are investigating the data breaches at Weil, Gotshal & Manges LLP and Cravath, Swaine & Moore LLP.[35]

Most notoriously, in April, 2016, public reports disclosed a massive leak of millions of documents and records from the Panama City-based law firm Mossack Fonseca. The leak exposed the business, financial, and tax dealings of thousands of world leaders, public figures, and popular celebrities as well as their global networks of friends, family members, and advisors. It has been described as the greatest data breach in history, at least of publicly reported ones within the private sector.

The implications of the Mossack Fonseca breach and the ensuing disclosures (the "Panama Papers") are still playing out legally, politically, and in the court of public opinion—and will for years to come. Depending upon their respective government's geopolitical posture, authorities around the world are now either gathering evidence for potential criminal cases against the firm and its clients or attempting to control (or "spin") the discussion about the significance of this information.

Putting aside questions about who was responsible for this hack and what its motivations were, experts quickly reached important conclusions about the nature of the attack:[36]

- The breach was long-standing—it went on for more than a year—and was discovered only when the stolen records were publicly disclosed.
- The outflow of client-sensitive information dated back to the 1970s and was voluminous, estimated at 4.2 million emails, three million database files, 2.1 million PDFs, 1.1 million images, 320,166 text files, and 2,242 files in other formats.
- The dissemination was continuous and widespread. There was a global appetite and capacity (and there is an ongoing effort) to analyze and further publicize the data as "newsworthy."
- The consequences to the firm and its clients will be long-term; investigations have been opened in numerous jurisdictions; and public disclosures are continuing.
- Most relevantly, Mossack Fonseca was not unique in relying upon antiquated and vulnerable information technology (IT) platforms, lax data and encryption protections, and outdated security access protocols.

According to authorities, the growing attacks on law enforcement entities also reflect the enhanced ability of actors to scour the digital landscape for sophisticated types of information and tools. In February, 2016, a posting appeared on an underground Russian

[33] *Id.*

[34] Nicole Hong & Robin Sidel, *Hackers Breach Law Firms, Including Cravath and Weil Gotshal*, Wall St. J. (Mar. 29, 2016), https://www.wsj.com/articles/hackers-breach-cravath-swaine-other-big-law-firms-1459293504.

[35] *Id.*

[36] *See* James Temperton & Matt Burgess, *Panama Papers: The Security Flaws at the Heart of Mossack Fonseca*, Wired UK (Apr. 6, 2016), http://www.wired.co.uk/news/archive/2016-04/06/panama-papers-mossack-fonseca-website-security-problems.

website called DarkMoney.cc in which someone offered to sell hacking services to other would-be cyber thieves and identified specific law firms as potential targets.[37] Of note, YouTube also hosts videos that offer hacking tutorials.[38]

Legal sector hackers, casting wide nets like commercial fishermen, often seek to gather large amounts of information indiscriminately and then analyze it later to see how it could be of value. This in turn can make it even more difficult to identify the responsible actors and the ultimate objectives of their attacks.

Understandably, entities in the legal sector, which comprises law firms, courts, and the service firms that support them, have become concerned about the obvious risks, and many have now taken matters into their own hands. Some clients are now asking for certifications about security, while others are conducting their own assessments of the firms they hire. Even major corporate clients that might not have questioned a law firm's cybersecurity practices independently are increasingly obligated to do so by government agencies such as the Securities and Exchange Commission's Office of Compliance Inspections and Examinations (OCIE).[39] The State of New York recognized the need for enhanced cybersecurity and was the first state to implement mandatory cybersecurity requirements on financial institutions. The regulation will require third-party vendors including law firms to be compliant with cybersecurity best practices.[40]

In response to this new phenomenon, some law firms now affirmatively disclose that they are compliant with cybersecurity standards such as ISO standard 27001.[41] Other law firms even view their investments in cybersecurity as a potential competitive advantage in attracting clients.[42]

Notwithstanding the material risks to attorney-client relationships—and the protection of communications, IP, business strategies, public market transactions, and sensitive governmental affairs—the legal sector, to date, has generally operated within a set of cybersecurity guidelines that has yet to give clear guidance about basic standards and best practices. (Note however that the ABA Model Rules of Professional Conduct have been updated, especially Rules 1.1 and 1.6, to address cybersecurity.)[43] Also, the Florida Supreme Court has recognized the need for increased awareness of cyber technology and

---

[37] *See generally* Hong & Sidel, *supra* note 34.

[38] Laurie Segall, *YouTube's "RAT" Problem*, CNN (July 29, 2015), https://money.cnn.com/2015/07/29/technology/youtube-ratting-problem/.

[39] Kenneth N. Rashbaum et al., *Cybersecurity: Business Imperative for Law Firms,* N.Y.L.J. (Dec. 10, 2014).

[40] Meghan Tribe, *As Cybersecurity hurdles loom, smaller firms face big challenges*, The Am. Lawyer. (Sept. 27, 2016), https://www.law.com/americanlawyer/almID/1202768670107/.

[41] Mary K. Pratt, *Law Firm Makes a Case for Security Certification,* CIO (Aug. 28, 2015), http://www.cio.com/article/2969323/security/law-firm-makes-a-case-for-security-certification.html.

[42] *See* ALM Media Properties, *Cybersecurity Ignorance Is Big Risk for Law Firms & Corporate Counsel, ALM Legal Intelligence Analysts Find,* ALM (Dec. 16, 2015), https://www.alm.com/press_release/cybersecurity-ignorance-is-big-risk-for-law-firms-corporate-counsel-alm-legal-intelligence-analysts-find/.

[43] Model Rules of Prof'l Conduct r. 1.1, cmt. 2 (Am. Bar Ass'n 2012) ("To maintain the requisite knowledge and skill, a lawyer should keep abreast of changes in the law and its practice, including the benefits and risks associated with relevant technology"); *see also id.* at r. 1.6(c) ("A lawyer shall make reasonable efforts to prevent the inadvertent or unauthorized disclosure of, or unauthorized access to, information relating to the representation of a client.").

security by requiring technology-related CLE courses.[44] As of this writing, its approach has not been followed by other jurisdictions.

Inevitably, cybersecurity standards for the legal sector will change, either voluntarily (e.g., through the American Bar Association), by regulation (e.g., through the Federal Trade Commission, the Department of Justice, the SEC, or State bar associations concerned with clients and liability claims), or because courts and court systems will demand that they change to protect the integrity of the rule of law. Until appropriate guidelines are set, however, it is essential for every entity engaged in the legal sector to understand and assess the nature of the exposures it faces. To this end, information sharing, benchmarking, and proactive thinking will be essential.

§ 3.04 THE RANGE OF SPECIFIC THREATS

As noted, hacks and intrusions can come from many sources and directions, including from state actors and foreign and domestic criminal networks seeking an easy means to steal valuable information. Notwithstanding their origins, most cyberattacks will fall into one of two main categories: human intent or mistake, and exploitation of software or hardware or both. The former category gains access to a system by exploiting information learned through acts of commission or omission by individuals who already have access to the system. The latter category seeks to gain access to systems through a vulnerability in a platform's security protocols, software, or hardware. The specific forms of exposures we will discuss include stolen and lost devices, employee criminality (the insider threat), social engineering, privilege abuse, bypassing of security controls, network port probes, unpatched software vulnerabilities, denial-of-service (DOS) attacks, group phishing, spear phishing, website exploits or browser security, bots, viruses and worms, Trojan horses, zero-day exploits, and spyware.

Again, it is important to keep in mind that attacks can be launched directly upon a court and its personnel, through litigants or their lawyers, or through vendors or suppliers. Courts must be particularly attuned to the controls in place with software suppliers, data storage providers, HR resources, and other platforms.

[A] Theft or Loss of a Device

The most common *reported* type of cyber breach experienced by courts is related to the loss or theft of a laptop, thumb drive, smartphone, tablet, or other mobile device.[45] If the information on the device was not encrypted, and if it contained or offered personally identifiable information, then a theft of information likely will occur. If the device lets

---

[44] Victor Li, *Florida Supreme Court Approves Mandatory Tech CLE Classes for Lawyers*, ABA Journal (Sept. 30, 2016), *available at* http://www.abajournal.com/news/article'florida_supreme_court_approves_mandatory_tech_cles_for_lawyers.

[45] Steve Couch, *Law Firm Exposure to Cyber Breach Threats*, Ohio Bar Liability Insurance Co., https://www.oblic.com/resources/06/09/2014/law-firm-exposure-to-cyber-breach-threats/.

the thief access court email and other court networks, such a theft or loss opens the door for cybercriminals to steal valuable information quickly.[46]

[B] Employee Criminality: The Insider Threat

Employee criminal activity (the insider threat) may pose a risk within the court environment.[47] The theft of a laptop, litigant or attorney data, or user identifications and passwords, or the introduction of various forms of malware and spyware can easily go undetected for a long period of time. Such conduct may originate with an employee or with an outside party who is able to "influence" an employee in a compromised position for any number of reasons.[48] By the time such conduct is discovered, the stolen data will often have made its way to third parties whose purposes can vary.[49] For this reason, as part of any cybersecurity measures, it may be advisable to conduct thorough and updated background checks of personnel.

[C] Social Engineering

Social engineering is defined as "an attack vector that relies heavily on human interaction and often involves tricking people into breaking normal security procedures."[50] A cyber attacker using social engineering will typically trick someone with access to the target computer system into divulging certain information (e.g., a password) that will enable the attacker to gain access to the system.[51] This technique can be used in isolation or combined with other cyber hostility modalities to achieve the attacker's goals. The danger of social engineering cannot be overstated: If an employee is tricked into revealing a password, a court can have all the best technological cybersecurity measures in place, only to have its entire regime rendered moot because of a socially-engineered breach.

---

[46] *Id.*

[47] *Id.*

[48] *Id.*

[49] *Id.*

[50] Margaret Rouse, *Social Engineering* (definition), TECH TARGET, http://searchsecurity.techtarget.com/definition/social-engineering.

[51] *See generally* Sherly Abraham & InduShobha Chengalur-Smith, *An Overview of Social Engineering Malware: Trends, Tactics, and Implications*, 32 TECH SOC'Y 123 (2010); *see also* Michael Workman, *Gaining Access with Social Engineering: An Empirical Study of the Threat*, 16 INFO. SYS. SEC. 315, 316 (2007).

Social engineers often attempt to persuade potential victims with appeals to their emotions such as excitement or fear; other times, they try to establish interpersonal relationships or create a feeling of trust and commitment. For example, they may promise a valuable prize or a financial interest in a transfer bank deposit if the victim complies with a request for bank account information. The emotional aspect of the interaction distracts people and serves to interfere with the potential victim's ability to carefully analyze the content of the message. *Id.*

[D] Insider or Privilege Abuse Hostilities

Insider or privilege-abuse hostilities occur when a court employee with a certain level of authorized access exceeds the scope of that authorization. In May, 2014, Ponemon Institute found that nearly half of the 693 corporations it surveyed did not have any policies for assigning privileged user-access.[52] Moreover, 88 percent of respondents felt that the risk of insider threats would continue to rise or stay the same.[53] Insider or privilege-abuse hostilities are incredibly difficult to defend against, as they involve parties who are trusted and authorized to access an entity's computer systems.[54] As a practical matter, it is incredibly difficult to monitor users effectively when they have authorized access, since such parties have regular access to confidential information.[55] Another possible complication in attempting to monitor users are the questions of who and how trustworthy the individual performing the monitoring is. This creates a situation where monitoring, as a security procedure, can become unproductive, inefficient, and wasteful.[56]

[E] Bypassing of Security Controls

Bypassing security controls, in the network security context, means that a hacker exploits "a flaw in a security system . . . to circumvent security mechanisms to get system or network access."[57] The key element in bypassing security controls is that the hacker, through a hardware device, a program, or a piece of code, can access the targeted system without having to go through the security clearance procedures the developer of the system implemented.[58] Bypass points are often referred to as *back doors* or *trap doors*.[59] Generally, back doors can be placed through two routes: either (1) by the original programmer, or (2) by a hacker implementing a system compromise such as a virus or worm.[60] A court may need to create a bypass in its system to allow authorized users

[52] *Privileged User Abuse & the Insider Threat*, PONEMON INSTITUTE (May 2014), http://www.raytheoncyber.com/rtnwcm/groups/cyber/documents/content/rtn_257010.pdf.

[53] *Id.*

[54] Frank L. Greitzer et al., *Combating the Insider Cyber Threat*, 6 IEEE SECURITY & PRIVACY 61, 61–64 (2002) ("The insider threat is manifested when human behavior departs from compliance with established policies, regardless of whether it results from malice or a disregard for security policies.").

[55] *Combating the Insider Threat*, U.S. COMP. EMERGENCY READINESS TEAM (last updated May 2, 2014), https://www.us-cert.gov/security-publications/Combating-Insider-Threat (attempting to give companies some guidance in being able to preempt, detect, and respond to insider/privilege-abuse hostilities).

[56] *See* Frank L. Greitzer & Deborah A. Frincke, *Combining Traditional Cyber Security Audit Data with Psychosocial Data: Towards Predictive Modeling for Insider Threat Mitigation*, INSIDER THREATS IN CYBER SECURITY 25 (Christian Probst et al., eds.), 2010 (proposing an alternative approach to internal threat monitoring that focuses on identifying potential insider threats before they become a problem).

[57] Margaret Rouse, *Bypass* [definition], TECH TARGET, http://searchsecurity.techtarget.com/definition/bypass.

[58] *Id.*

[59] A *back door* is an undocumented "means of [accessing] a computer program that bypasses security mechanisms." Margaret Rouse, *Back Door* [definition], TECH TARGET, http://searchsecurity.techtarget.com/definition/back-door.

[60] *Id.*

to circumvent normal security procedures.[61] Hackers, in contrast, use back doors for easier and continued access to a system after an initial compromise.[62]

Sometimes, rather than focusing on access to a computer system, hackers may only want to access the data stored within that system. Then they will seek what is referred to as a *crypto bypass*. A crypto bypass is a flaw that allows for circumvention of normally required data-encryption processes for exporting data so that the data remains in plain-text form.[63]

[F] Network Port Probes

A *port* is "nothing more than an integer that uniquely identifies an endpoint of a communication stream."[64] The easiest way to conceptualize a port is like a phone number extension, except that every phone number uses the exact same extensions (e.g., extension 100 gets you the master voice mailbox on every 200 number around the globe). A computer can have up to 65,535 ports,[65] each dedicated to a specific function. Ports also work to divide computer processes, since only one process (e.g., email) can operate on a given port. A hacker that performs a network port scan essentially sends a series of messages to every port on a computer system in an attempt to discern which processes correspond to which ports. This gives the hacker an idea of where a computer system may be most vulnerable. For example, a hacker may use a port scan to discover that an email port has no password protection, and then seek to exploit that weakness in a potential attack. It is important to understand that even though a port scan may not directly cause harm to a computer system, it is a critical reconnaissance step that will inform how a hacker will carry out an attack and what sorts of cyber hostilities the hacker is likely to employ.

[G] Unpatched Software Vulnerabilities

An unpatched software vulnerability "is a security flaw, glitch, or weakness found in software or in an operating system (OS) that can lead to security concerns" through the

---

[61] *Id.*

[62] Selvakumar, *Bypass Authentication*, Knox, http://knoxd3.blogspot.com/2014/01/bypass-authentication.html. Negligence, ignorance, or simple understatement of security threats often result in authentication schemes that can be bypassed by simply skipping the login page and directly calling an internal page that is supposed to be accessed only after authentication has been performed. In addition to this, it is often possible to bypass authentication measures by tampering with requests and tricking the application into thinking that the user is already authenticated. This can be accomplished by modifying the given URL parameter, by manipulating the form, or by counterfeiting sessions. *Id.*

[63] Rouse, *Bypass*, *supra* note 56.

[64] *Glossary of Security Terms*, SANS, https://www.sans.org/security-resources/glossary-of-terms/?pass=w.

[65] Margaret Rouse, *Port* [definition], Tech Target, http://searchnetworking.techtarget.com/definition/port.

use of an exploit by a hacker.[66] (*Exploits* are discussed below.) Software and operating system developers, who try to create a product without flaws, constantly struggle against hackers, who never stop searching for any imperfection they can use to exploit the software and gain access to the computer system.

There are many known types of software vulnerabilities,[67] and more are always being discovered. To understand how this type of cyber hostility functions, take for example one of the most common software vulnerabilities: a buffer overflow.[68] A buffer overflow "occurs when a program or process tries to store more data in a buffer (temporary data storage area) than the buffer was intended to hold. Since buffers are meant to contain a limited amount of data, the extra information—which has to go somewhere—can overflow into adjacent buffers, corrupting or overwriting the valid data held in them."[69] Cybercriminals will attempt to exploit a buffer overflow in order to gain unauthorized access to a court's computer system.[70] Buffer overflows, like other software vulnerabilities, are typically the result of poor software construction; but fortunately, they are not permanent. A court can apply a software "patch"[71] to fix whatever poor lines of code led to the vulnerability.

Vulnerabilities are found in nearly every substantial piece of software including operating systems, which is why public and private entities are constantly looking for vulnerabilities and releasing patches. For example, on the second Tuesday of every month, Microsoft releases patches for all newly identified vulnerabilities. This tradition has come to be known as "Patch Tuesday."[72] Once Microsoft releases its patch to the public, users are expected to update their systems with the new patches.[73] These patches remedy whatever vulnerability was detected in the software. However, they are effective only if installed, and many users unfortunately do not actively update their software on a regular basis with the newest patches. This creates a far bigger threat than just the latent vulnerability itself. A patch in the hands of a cybercriminal is an easy-to-use instruction manual on how to exploit the software vulnerabilities found in unpatched systems.

---

[66] *Gateways to Infection: Exploiting Software Vulnerabilities*, TrendMicro (Sep. 3, 2012), https://www.trendmicro.com/vinfo/us/threat-encyclopedia/web-attack/129/gateways-to-infection-exploiting-software-vulnerabilities.

[67] *Common Weakness Enumeration,* CWE-2000: Comprehensive CWE Dictionary, https://cwe.mitre.org/data/slices/2000.html.

[68] *Gateways to Infection*, *supra* note 65.

[69] Margaret Rouse, *Buffer Overflow* [definition], Tech Target, http://searchsecurity.techtarget.com/definition/buffer-overflow; *see also Gateways to Infection, supra* note 66.

[70] Rouse, *supra* note 62. Although it may occur accidentally through a programming error, buffer overflow is an increasingly common type of security attack on data integrity. In buffer overflow attacks, the extra data may contain codes designed to trigger specific actions, in effect sending new instructions to the attacked computer that could, for example, damage the user's files, change data, or disclose confidential information. Buffer overflow attacks are said to have arisen because the C programming language supplied the framework, and poor programming practices supplied the vulnerability.

[71] Margaret Rouse, *Patch (fix)* [definition], Tech Target, http://searchenterprisedesktop.techtarget.com/definition/patch.

[72] Margaret Rouse, *Patch Tuesday* [definition], Tech Target, http://searchsecurity.techtarget.com/definition/Patch-Tuesday.

[73] *Id.*

[H] Denial-of-Service Attacks

A *denial-of-service attack* (a DOS attack) is defined as "the prevention of authorized access to a system resource or the delaying of system operations and functions."[74] DOS attacks attempt to overload a computer system by forcing an improper allocation of resources through bulk accessing of a network connection.[75] The basis of a DOS attack is akin to someone ringing your front doorbell and then running away: While you are answering the door, you are unable to do anything else. In the world of high-speed communications, a hacker can ring your digital doorbell millions of times a second and force your computer system to do nothing but answer the door, leaving it no time to perform legitimate functions such as email.[76]

[I] Group Phishing

Phishing is an attempt—usually perpetrated through email by someone masquerading as a legitimate entity—to steal your personal information.[77] Hackers often send these fake emails by the thousands (which is referred to as *group phishing*). A phishing email will generally claim that the sender is a well-known organization the target may or may not have a relationship with, and that the organization needs personal information such as the target's credit card or social security number, usernames, passwords, or some combination of these. This information is generally not collected in the email; rather, the message almost always contains a link asking the target to access a website in order to relay the information.[78] Importantly, because group phishing relies on large numbers, time is of the essence to hackers as the most recently stolen identities command the highest prices.[79]

---

[74] *Glossary of Security Terms*, SANS, *available at* http://www.sans.org/security-resources/glossary-of-terms.

[75] *See Understanding Denial-of-Service Attacks*, U.S. Comp. Emergencyt Readness Team, https://www.us-cert.gov/ncas/tips/ST04-015. In a denial-of-service attack, an attacker attempts to prevent legitimate users from accessing information or services. By targeting your computer and its network connection, or the computers and network of the sites you are trying to use, an attacker may be able to prevent you from accessing email, websites, online accounts (for banking, etc.), or other services that rely on the affected computer.

[76] *Id.* ("By sending many, or large, email messages to the account, an attacker can consume your quota, preventing you from receiving legitimate messages.").

[77] *What Is Phishing?*, Phish Tank, https://www.phishtank.com/what_is_phishing.php; *see also* Margaret Rouse, *phishing* [definition], Tech Target, http://searchsecurity.techtarget.com/definition/phishing.

[78] *Online Fraud: Phishing*, Norton, http://us.norton.com/cybercrime-phishing.

[79] *See Phishing: A Very Dangerous Cyber Threat*, InfoSec Inst. (Dec. 13, 2012), https://resources.infosecinstitute.com/phishing-dangerous-cyber-threat/#gref. ("The total loss for various organizations comes to $2.1 billion over the last 12 months. RSA estimates that there have been nearly 33,000 phishing attacks each month worldwide this year; countries such as Canada have registered an increase of 400 percent in the number of attacks.").

[J] Spear Phishing

Unlike group phishing, and as the name suggests, *spear phishing* is a targeted, individually designed phishing attempt. The goal of a spear-phishing attack is to gain access or spread malware to a specific system, typically not to steal an identity but rather to steal intellectual property, financial data, trade secrets, military secrets, or court or other confidential data.[80] Hackers may use any available means to make their phishing attempt as effective as possible. For example, the FBI has warned of spear-phishing scams in which the emails appeared to be from the National Center for Missing & Exploited Children.[81] It only takes one momentary lapse in judgment caused by an emotionally charged email for this kind of attack to succeed, so spear phishing is incredibly dangerous and incredibly difficult to guard against.

[K] Website Exploits and Browser Security

Web browsers—such as Internet Explorer, Mozilla Firefox, and Apple Safari (to name a few)—are ubiquitous on all computers that an organization would use.[82] Hence they have become an increasingly popular route of attack for hackers,[83] as these browsers will usually not have been properly configured to maximize security. "Often, the web browser that comes with an operating system is not set up in a secure default configuration. Not securing a web browser can lead quickly to a variety of computer problems ranging from spyware being installed to intruders taking control of the computer."[84]

---

[80] *Id.* ("Spear phishing attempts are not typically initiated by 'random hackers' but are more likely to be conducted by perpetrators out for financial gain, trade secrets or military information.").

[81] Darrell Foxworth, *FBI Warns of Spear-Phishing E-Mail with Missing Children Theme*, Fed. Buerau of Inv. (Aug. 26, 2013), http://www.fbi.gov/sandiego/press-releases/2013/fbi-warns-of-spear-phishing-e-mail-with-missing-children-theme ("The subject of the e-mail is 'Search for Missing Children,' and a zip file containing three malicious files is attached. E-mail recipients should never open attachments or click links in suspicious e-mails.").

[82] *Securing Your Web Browser*, U.S. Comp. Emergency Readiness Team, https://www.us-cert.gov/publications/securing-your-web-browser.

[83] *Id.*

[84] *Id.* ("Attackers focus on exploiting client-side systems (your computer) through various vulnerabilities. They use these vulnerabilities to take control of your computer, steal your information, destroy your files, and use your computer to attack other computers. A low-cost way attackers do this is by exploiting vulnerabilities in web browsers.").

This problem is made worse by a number of factors, including the following nine items:

(1) Many users have a tendency to click on links without considering the risks of their actions.
(2) Web page addresses can be disguised or take you to an unexpected site.
(3) Many web browsers are configured to provide increased functionality at the cost of decreased security.
(4) New security vulnerabilities are often discovered after the software is configured and packaged by the manufacturer.
(5) Computer systems and software packages may be bundled with additional software, which increases the number of vulnerabilities that may be attacked.
(6) Third-party software may not have a mechanism for receiving security updates.

[L] Bots and Command & Control Centers

A *bot*, "derived from the word 'robot', is a program that operates as an agent for a user or another program or simulates a human activity."[85] Bots can be used to perform a wide range of functions that a human would otherwise perform, ranging from automated tasks to providing information.[86] Bots generally serve to collect information (as is the case with web crawlers) but can also be used to interact automatically with web interfaces such as Internet messaging.[87]

Bots can be used for either good or malicious purposes. An example of a good bot is Googlebot, a program created by Google in order to index all websites on the Internet.[88] Malicious bots attempt to access computer systems and engage in self-propagation in order to infect many systems. These systems are then linked back to a command and control (C&C) center so that the hacker can use them all as a network of compromised devices known as a "botnet."[89]

With a botnet, hackers can use a multitude of bots to engage in flood-type attacks against their targets. Botnets can employ a wide gamut of malware programs, making this type of cyberattack very flexible. Bots may be able to log keystrokes, collect passwords, capture and analyze packets, gather financial information, launch DOS attacks, relay spam, and open back doors on the infected host.[90] Because bots are so versatile, they can easily be modified within hours of their identification by antimalware companies.[91] Furthermore, bots can take advantage of back doors that have been created by worms and viruses, which gives them the potential to infect even the most secure computer systems.[92]

---

(7) Many websites require that users enable certain features or install more software, putting the computer at additional risk.

(8) Many users do not know how to configure their web browsers securely.

(9) Many users are unwilling to enable or disable functionality as required to secure their web browser.

[85] Margaret Rouse, *Bot (robot)* [definition], TECH TARGET (May 26, 2015), https://searchmicroservices.techtarget.com/definition/bot-robot.

[86] *What Is the Difference: Viruses, Worms, Trojans, and Bots?*, CISCO, https://www.cisco.com/c/en/us/about/security-center/virus-differences.html; *see generally* MARKUS JAKOBSSON & ZULFIKAR RAMZAN, CRIMEWARE: UNDERSTANDING NEW ATTACKS AND DEFENSES (2002).

[87] *What Is the Difference: Viruses, Worms, Trojans, and Bots?, CISCO, https://www.cisco.com/c/en/us/about/security-center/virus-differences.html*

[88] *Googlebot*, BOTOPEDIA, http://www.botopedia.org/user-agent-list/search-bots/googlebot.

[89] Nyakundi Elijah, *Computer Viruses and Their Effects*, NYASOFT (Feb. 1, 2015), http://nyasoft.blogspot.com/2015/02/computer-viruses-and-their-effects.html; Chunyong Yin et al., *Botnet Detection Based on Correlation of Malicious Behaviors*, 6 INT'L J. HYBRID INFO. TECH. 291, 293 (2013), http://www.sersc.org/journals/IJHIT/vol6_no6_2013/26.pdf. ("Bot infection usually occurs through trapped files, e-mail attachments or web pages. However, trend in bot technology includes a blending of Trojan-horse, virus, worm, and backdoor functionality.").

[90] *What Is the Difference?*, *supra* note 86.

[91] *See* KEN DUNHAM & JIM MELNICK, MALICIOUS BOTS: AN INSIDE LOCK INTO THE CYBER-CRIMINAL UNDER-GROUND OF THE INTERNET 2 (2002).

[92] *Id.*

[M] Viruses and Worms

A computer *virus* "is a program or programming code that replicates by being copied or initiating its copying to another program, computer boot sector or document."[93] Viruses are capable of spreading from computer to computer and from network to network, leaving a trail of infected systems as they travel. Viruses can have a wide variety of effects, ranging in severity from causing annoyance, to damaging data or software, to denial-of-service conditions.[94] Most viruses are code that is added onto an executable file, which means that a virus can lie dormant in a system but not become active or able to spread until the host file is executed.[95] Once the host file is executed, the virus is activated.[96] Viruses often do not prevent the host file from running as usual,[97] but some are coded in such a way as to delete a computer's files—including the host file—upon execution.[98]

A computer *worm* "is a self-replicating virus that does not alter files but resides in active memory and duplicates itself."[99] Computer worms are similar to viruses in that they replicate functional copies of themselves and can cause the same type of damage.[100] Whereas viruses require the spreading of an infected host file, worms are stand-alone software and do not require a host program or a human to help with their propagation.[101] In order to spread, worms must exploit a vulnerability in a computer system or use social engineering to exploit the users of a target system.[102] Worms function by taking advantage of file- or information-transport features in a computer system which allow the worm to travel unaided.[103]

[N] Trojan Horses

A *Trojan horse* "is a program in which malicious or harmful code is contained inside apparently harmless programming or data in such a way that it can get control and do its

---

[93] Margaret Rouse, *Virus* [definition], Tech Target (May 26, 2015), https://searchsecurity.techtarget.com/definition/virus/.

[94] *What Is a Computer Virus or a Computer Worm?*, Kaspersky, https://usa.kaspersky.com/resource-center/threats/computer-viruses-vs-worms. ("Computer worms can exploit network configuration errors (for example, to copy themselves onto a fully accessible disk) or exploit loopholes in operating system and application security. Many worms will use more than one method in order to spread copies via networks.").

[95] *What Is the Difference?, supra* note 86.

[96] *Id.*

[97] *See* Alan Solomon, *All About Viruses*, VX Heaven, http://vxheaven.org/lib/aas10.html.

[98] *Id.*

[99] Margaret Rouse, *Worm* [definition], Tech Target (May 26, 2015), http://searchsecurity.techtarget.com/definition/worm.

[100] *Computer Worms*, Tech FAQ, http://www.tech-faq.com/computer-worm.html (last updated Nov. 26, 2013).

[101] *Id.*

[102] *What Is the Difference?, supra* note 86.

[103] *Id.*

chosen form of damage."[104] The danger of Trojan horses is that the software will look legitimate to a user who actually has been tricked into loading and executing a malicious piece of code.[105] Trojan horses can have a wide variety of effects, including irritating users (e.g., with pop-up windows), damaging the computer system (e.g., by deleting files or spreading other malware), or developing a back door which a hacker can later use to gain easy access to the computer system.[106]

[O] Zero-Day Exploits

An *exploit* is when a hacker uses a piece of software, command, or methodology to take advantage of a particular security vulnerability.[107] An exploit only confirms whether a vulnerability exists. In other words, an exploit is not inherently malicious; but in the hands of a bad actor, it can be used to devastating effect.[108] Additionally, exploits are a common component found in malware.

To combat exploits, security vendors study known exploits and identify them based on their content and behavior while executing.[109] These vendors then categorize exploits based on identified indicators of compromise (IOCs);[110] such IOCs are included in "known signature" databases which are continually updated with the newest *identified* exploits. However, security vendors are helpless against a *zero-day exploit*, one "that takes advantage of a security vulnerability on the same day that the vulnerability becomes generally known."[111] These exploits are essentially impossible to detect until they have been caught, identified, analyzed for new IOCs, and added to known signature databases.[112]

---

[104] Margaret Rouse, *Trojan horse* [definition], Tech Target (May 26, 2015), http://searchsecurity.techtarget.com/definition/Trojan-horse.

[105] *Crimeware: Trojans and Spyware*, Norton, http://us.norton.com/cybercrime-trojansspyware. Increasingly, Trojans are the first stage of an attack, and their primary purpose is to stay hidden while downloading and installing a stronger threat, such as a bot. Unlike viruses and worms, Trojan horses cannot spread by themselves. They are often delivered to a victim through an email in which it masquerades as an image or joke, or through a malicious website which installs the Trojan horse on a computer through vulnerabilities in web-browser software, such as Microsoft Internet Explorer. *Id.*

[106] "Trojan horses are broken down in classification based on how they breach systems and the damage they cause." Vangie Beal, *Trojan Horse*, Webopedia, http://www.webopedia.com/TERM/T/Trojan_horse.html (providing an analysis of the various classifications of Trojan horse).

[107] Margaret Rouse, *Exploit* [definition], Tech Target (May 26, 2015), http://searchsecurity.techtarget.com/definition/exploit.

[108] *What Is the Difference? supra* note 86.

[109] *See generally* Leyla Bilge & Tudor Dumitras, *Before We Knew It: An Empirical Study of Zero-Day Attacks in the Real World*, *in* Proc. of the 2012 ACM Conference on Computer & Comm. 233–44 (2012).

[110] An IOC is an artifact observed on a network or in an operating system that indicates a computer intrusion with high confidence. Typical IOCs are virus signatures and IP addresses, MD5 hashes of malware files or URLs, or domain names of botnet command and control servers.

[111] Margaret Rouse, *Zero-Day Exploit* [definition], Tech Target (July 2010), http://searchsecurity.techtarget.com/definition/zero-day-exploit.

[112] Elizabeth Palermo, *What Is a Zero-Day Exploit?*, Tom's Guide (Nov. 22, 2013, 4:56 PM), http://www.tomsguide.com/us/zero-day-exploit-definition,news-17903.html ("The most dangerous varieties of

[P] Spyware

Spyware is "any technology that aids in gathering information about a person or organization without their knowledge."[113] Spyware can take many different forms. For example, spyware can appear as one or more programs that monitor what a user does online (sometimes referred to as a *spybot*) and thereby gather information without having to be installed on the computer system. Often, these types of spyware are not necessarily used for malicious purposes but rather to gather information about users in order to sell the aggregated information to advertisers or other interested parties.[114] Spyware can also be placed locally onto a computer as a software virus or as the result of installing a new program.[115] Since users not infrequently agree to allow an installed software to monitor some of their data, not all data-collecting programs are spyware; but it is improper unless the user knows what data is being collected and with whom it is being shared.[116] Spyware differs from these programs because it is installed without the user's consent and generally without an awareness of even having downloaded it. Often, users will unintentionally download spyware through an action as simple as clicking an option in a deceptive pop-up window.

§ 3.05 CONCLUSION

Cyber threats are rapidly growing. They are one of our most significant exposures to a rapidly expanding universe of incentivized actors and conspirators: organized criminals, state or state-sponsored actors, terrorists, and hacktivists, to name a few. New forms of cyber hostilities arise daily, and new technologies for launching these attacks will continuously develop and evolve.

We should expect our adversaries to wage information operations against the justice system by penetrating courts' computer networks or judges' personal email accounts to expose derogatory communications or to mix in fabricated ones; to steal sensitive data; to alter release orders or even falsify drafts of opinions; or just to demonstrate that the networks can be hacked. Many have noted that the best way to counter false information is to make the public aware that there are those who want to deceive them. Opponents of our judicial system want to exploit the decline of trust in our democratic institutions. The

---

zero-day exploits facilitate drive-by downloads, in which simply browsing to an exploited Web page or clicking a poisoned Web link can result in a full-fledged malware attack on your system. Such attacks exploit vulnerabilities within a Web browser's software, or within third-party browser plug-ins.").

[113] Margaret Rouse, *Spyware* [definition], TECH TARGET, http://searchsecurity.techtarget.com/definition/spyware.

[114] *Id.*

[115] *Id.*; *see also* Beal, *Spyware, supra* note 99 ("Spyware is similar to a Trojan horse in that users unwittingly install the product when they install something else. A common way to become a victim of spyware is to download certain peer-to-peer file swapping products that are available today.").

[116] Rouse, *supra* note 106; Beal, *supra* note 99 ("Licensing agreements that accompany software downloads sometimes warn the user that a spyware program will be installed along with the requested software, but the licensing agreements may not always be read completely because the notice of a spyware installation is often couched in obtuse, hard-to-read legal disclaimers.").

judiciary must be prepared to respond quickly, and attorneys must be prepared to help set the record straight when misinformation floods public discourse.

As a result, it is now incumbent upon judiciary systems to understand what makes them a potentially attractive target and to know the varied and multifarious nature of the threats. To this end, knowledge-sharing and benchmarking will be essential components in the formulation of an effective, risk-based approach to protecting the security and confidentiality of court information.

Although the discussion in this chapter does not exhaustively list or comprehensively describe all the intricacies of the existing threats in the cyber realm, we hope it will serve as a useful introduction to the most common and prevalent threats that courts and judiciary-wide systems are likely to face, and to the behaviors of those who will attack their IT systems.

CHAPTER 4

WHAT IT TAKES TO FRUSTRATE THE HACKER KNOCKING AT YOUR DOOR

Daniel Garrie, Esq., Judge Leo M. Gordon, Greg Kelley, Richard Rushing, and Bill Spernow

§ 4.01 Do Not Be the Low-Hanging Fruit

§ 4.02 Proper Password Management Is Essential to Security

§ 4.03 Firewalls: Regulating Who and What Can Access Your System

§ 4.04 Applying Patches: Keeping Your Software as Secure and Up-to-Date as Possible

§ 4.05 Perimeter Security Controls: What It Takes to Keep the Bad Guys Out

§ 4.06 Encryption

§ 4.07 Summary

It is often said that water takes the path of least resistance. This is equally true of hackers seeking to break into court computer systems. This chapter discusses methods and practices to frustrate these hackers.

§ 4.01 DO NOT BE THE LOW-HANGING FRUIT

What many public and private entities today do not realize is that everyone is a target.[1] You may be a target because of who you interact with, the information you have, the litigants who have come under your jurisdiction, or the simple fact that you are on the Internet. So, how do you go about protecting yourself? One of the easiest ways is to prevent yourself from being one of the many low-hanging fruits. What does that mean? This chapter discusses ways to avoid being an easy target.

§ 4.02 PROPER PASSWORD MANAGEMENT IS ESSENTIAL TO SECURITY

Millions of passwords or password equivalents are stolen every year and used by attackers to comprise organizations.

One of the first and best ways to avoid being low-hanging fruit is proper password management. To understand password management, let us examine how passwords are stored in a Windows environment. In Windows, the password is not stored in plain text; instead, the hash of a password is stored. Some of you reading this may have heard the word *hash* in the context of computer forensics, and the term is used similarly here.[2] To create a hash, the password is put through a mathematical formula; the result is a series of letters and numbers that represent the password. The workings of the formula mean that you cannot turn the hash back into a password. Thus, when you enter your password into your Windows computer, that password is put through the same hash-formula, and the result is compared to the stored hash of your password. If the hashes match, then the password you entered is considered to match the stored password, and you are allowed to log into or onto your computer.

Windows allows both uppercase and lowercase letters as well as numbers and punctuation symbols to be included in a password. With that set of characters, there are 6,634,204,312,890,625 possible different passwords if one restricts the length of the password to eight characters. Hackers are often left to "brute-force crack" a password, which means that they have to try all of those combinations until they are successful. If hackers could enter a password every second, it would still take them 210 million years to guess. So you think you are safe? Not really. In 2012, Jeremi Gosney of Stricture Consulting Group created a computer that was able to guess 350 billion passwords per second.[3] As

[1] Kim Zetter, *Everyone Has Been Hacked. Now What?*, Wired (May 4, 2012), http://www.wired.com/2012/05/everyone-hacked/.

[2] Alan G. Konhem, *Hashing for Storage: Data Management*, in Hashing in Computer Science: Fifty Years of Slicing and Dicing (2010).

[3] Dan Goodin, *25-GPU Cluster Cracks Every Standard Windows Password in <6 Hours*, Ars Technica (Dec. 9, 2012), https://arstechnica.com/information-technology/2012/12/25-gpu-cluster-cracks-every-standard-windows-password-in-6-hours/.

a result, he could crack any eight-character Windows password in less than six hours. Not so safe now, are we? Well, consider this: If we used 10 characters for our passwords—a mere two more characters—Gosney's machine would take five-and-a-half years to crack them.

Of course, Mr. Gosney's research was done in 2012. Machines and password-cracking methods have evolved since then. Still, realize that password-cracking routines need to try over and over with different passwords to be successful, and Windows has a built-in prevention mechanism to prevent anyone from repeatedly trying passwords. You can set Windows to lock an account after any number of consecutively entered bad passwords.[4] A good rule of thumb is five bad passwords in a row, meaning the account is locked after five guesses. When the account is locked, it no longer allows anyone to log into the account. That action has two results: First, the hacker cannot make any more password guesses until the account is unlocked or a specific length of time (maybe 30 minutes) has passed. Second, the person who (legitimately) uses the account immediately finds out that they cannot use it anymore. This person reports the lock-out to the IT department, which then is alerted to the possibility that someone is trying to hack the account.

Another great weapon against brute-force attacks is to *change your password frequently*.[5] If a hacker is trying to brute-force attack your password and you change it, in essence that forces the hacker to start all over again at guessing passwords. Changing passwords monthly is a good idea but can sometimes be a bit much for most users. A change every 90 days (four times a year) should strike a good balance between being a nuisance and practicing good password management.

Proper password management also means training your users to set good passwords. So far, we have been talking about a brute-force attack (guessing all combinations of letters and numbers). Another and sometimes the easier method is called a *dictionary attack*.[6] Hackers are known to start guessing passwords by trying words from the dictionary. Sometimes that will include foreign-language dictionaries as well. Think you are smart by changing the letter "I" to a "1" or the letter "S" to a "$" in your password? That is called password "munging." Hackers compensate for munging nowadays as well. The best advice here is to forget dictionary words. Many times organizations have issues with users picking revolving passwords, such as "Spring2018" that will be changed to "Summer2018." Sometimes these passwords leak, as they are often used not only for the organizational account itself but also for any Internet application for which the user has to create an account.

Unfortunately, users often find themselves at a loss to remember complex passwords, such that many resort to writing them down on a sticky note and sticking it to their monitors. If an organization allows that to occur, it might as well return to using passwords

[4] *Account Lockout Threshold*, Microsoft: Technet (July 17, 2014), https://technet.microsoft.com/en-us/library/hh994574.aspx.

[5] Melissa Cocks, *The Importance of Changing Passwords,* NSK (Oct. 2, 2009), http://blog.nskinc.com/topic/data-security/IT-Services-Boston/The-Importance-of-Changing-Passwords.

[6] Dan Goodin, *Why Passwords Have Never Been Weaker—and Crackers Have Never Been Stronger*, Ars Technica (Aug. 20, 2012), *available at* http://arstechnica.com/security/2012/08/passwords-under-assault/.

like "1234." The solution for remembering passwords is a password management application.[7] Many password management applications are available, and many of them are free. Some are web-based, so that users can access their passwords from multiple locations. The use of a password-protected Word document or Excel spreadsheet is also acceptable.

Some organizations still tolerate the most egregious violation of sound security hygiene: password sharing.[8] The biggest problem with this practice is that it removes all accountability for actions in an environment. If multiple people know the password to one's account, it is exceedingly difficult to ascribe blame properly when that account is used in an unauthorized fashion. All too often, computer forensics investigations grind to a screeching halt because investigators determine that multiple people had access to the account in question, and that it is therefore impossible to determine who was responsible for the offending action. Some organizations feel the need to have users share passwords with their IT department. That practice too is unnecessary. Proper planning would allow IT to get into any device through the ability to reset a password.

Proper password management extends to mobile devices. While "bring your own device" (BYOD) is prevalent today, it does not stop a company from extending its password policies to those mobile devices.[9] In fact, since the 2003 version, Microsoft Exchange has had a built-in feature that allows a company to force mobile devices to be encrypted, to require a password of a certain length, and to force users to change that password.[10] So, needless to say, password management can and should be implemented on all mobile devices.

Another thing to keep in mind is that brute-force password cracking works best when the database containing the hashes is stolen. Once stolen, the hashes can be brute-force cracked offline without any detection. Therefore, proper protection of your computers to prevent the theft of hashes is important. (This is discussed later.)

To summarize, implement and practice the following password policies:

1. Ignore words from the dictionary.
2. Use passwords at least 10 characters long; the bigger the better; and remember that computers always get more powerful with each passing year.
3. Implement a lockout policy in your environment to catch brute-force attempts.
4. Change your passwords every 90 days (four times per year).

---

[7] April Glaser, *You Need a Password Manager. Here Are Some Good Free Ones*, Wired (Jan. 24, 2016), http://www.wired.com/2016/01/you-need-a-password-manager/; David Silver et al., *Password Managers: Attacks and Defenses,* USENIX (Aug. 2014), https://www.usenix.org/system/files/conference/usenixsecurity 14/sec14-paper-silver.pdf.

[8] Monica Whitty et al., *Individual Differences in Cyber Security Behaviors: An Examination of Who Is Sharing Passwords*, 18 Cyberpsychol. Behav. Soc. Networks 3 (Jan. 2015), http://www.ncbi.nlm.nih.gov/pmc/articles/PMC4291202/.

[9] Nate Lord, *BYOD Security: Expert Tips on Policy, Mitigating Risks, & Preventing a Breach*, Digital Guardian (Jan. 12, 2016), https://digitalguardian.com/blog/byod-security-expert-tips-policy-mitigating-risks-preventing-breach.

[10] *Id.*

5. Do not ignore or exclude mobile devices.
6. Do not ignore or exclude administrative accounts running on servers.

§ 4.03 FIREWALLS: REGULATING WHO AND WHAT CAN ACCESS YOUR SYSTEM

Now that we have talked about passwords, let us discuss another area where you can keep from being the low-hanging fruit: Public and private entities large and small should implement a firewall and put some very simple, basic, and effective controls in place.

What is a firewall? Basically, a *firewall* is a device that sits between your network and the Internet. A firewall acts as a gateway or a traffic cop, monitoring communication going between your environment and the rest of the world.[11] A firewall can deny traffic, allow traffic, or just monitor and log traffic. Some are simple: Plug them in, make some configuration changes, and let them go. Others are more complex, requiring hours to configure properly.

One common misstep for many people is neglecting to implement the same password controls on the firewall. The most egregious violations are when people do not change the out-of-the-box password for the administrative account. Many times this is the first thing an attacker may try to compromise. A November, 2014 article in *Network World* discussed a website that broadcasted more than 73,000 Internet-accessible cameras.[12] How were the hackers able to do that? They just used the default passwords for each camera, connected, and started broadcasting. A properly functioning firewall would block a hacker from broadcasting anything. However, if the default password on a firewall is not changed, the hackers will instead use that account to give themselves an open door to come into the court's network and steal whatever they want.

After changing your default password, the next step to consider with firewalls is stopping traffic coming into the court's environment. The stopping or allowing of traffic is usually done by disabling or enabling different ports. Everyone is familiar with an Internet Protocol (IP) address.[13] IP addresses are used to communicate with other devices by any device such as your computer when it is connected to the Internet or any network. (Think of an IP address as a phone number or house address.) However, each device also listens on specific ports for communication.[14] Web servers listen on port 80 for regular traffic and on port 443 for encrypted (https://) traffic.[15] What does that mean? When a computer browses a website, it is of course communicating with the IP address of that

---

[11] Kenneth Ingham & Stephanie Forrest, *A History and Survey of Network Firewalls* (Technical Report TR-CS-2002-37), University of New Mexico (2002), http://www.cs.unm.edu/~treport/tr/02-12/firewall.pdf.

[12] Ms. Smith, *Peeping into 73,000 Unsecured Security Cameras Thanks to Default Passwords*, Network World (Nov. 6, 2014), https://www.csoonline.com/article/2844283/peeping-into-73-000-unsecured-security-cameras-thanks-to-default-passwords.html.

[13] *Understanding IP Addressing: Everything You Ever Wanted to Know*, 3 Com (2001), http://pages.di.unipi.it/ricci/501302.pdf.

[14] *Network Port*, Techopedia, https://www.techopedia.com/definition/24717/network-port.

[15] *Service Name and Transport Protocol Port Number Registry*, Iana (last updated Apr. 7, 2016), https://www.iana.org/assignments/service-names-port-numbers/service-names-port-numbers.txt.

website; but it is doing so on port 80 or port 443, depending on whether the communication is unencrypted or encrypted. If your email server is sending email to another server, it contacts that other server on port 25.

To bring it back to the firewall, for small court offices with no email, web, or other servers that need to communicate with the outside world, the setup is quite easy: block all incoming traffic. For other environments that do have external-facing servers such as an email server, a common practice is to start with enabling only what a court needs. A court can stop or allow traffic not only to certain IP addresses but also to certain ports.[16] That means if a court has an email server in its network, best practice is not to allow all port traffic to that server but only traffic to port 25, the one for email traffic. A best practice in firewall setup is to open up only those IP addresses and ports that are needed for communication, and to disable everything else. Over time, a court may have to open up more ports as it increases its services; but do not neglect the concept of closing ports as time goes by and services are discontinued. If you make a switch and start using email in the cloud, turn off the traffic to the court's email server. One common mistake in many environments is to allow traffic through the firewall and directly to a server for the purpose of using Remote Desktop[17] or other "trouble shooting" applications. That policy serves only to open up an unnecessary vulnerability. A more appropriate method for connecting to an internal server via Remote Desktop would be to establish a virtual private network (VPN) connection instead.[18] A VPN will allow remote users to communicate on the court's network as if they were sitting in the courthouse. The network traffic over a VPN is encrypted and secure. Once on a VPN, users can then connect to whatever server or computer they desire through Remote Destop.

Firewall selection is also important. Though it is not recommended, one may encounter an email or web server being used for the dual purpose of a firewall. Understand that the court's firewall is going to receive the brunt of network traffic and attacks.[19] If a court is also using its firewall as an email server, it creates an extra service burden that can weaken the firewall, compromise its effectiveness, and jeopardize the security of the court's systems. The best practice is to use a dedicated device that serves only one purpose: acting as a firewall. Preferably, the device should have originally been designed as a firewall; this is better than taking a server and making it into a firewall.

---

[16] Ed Bott, *Lock IT Down: Block TCP/IP Ports to Increase Security*, TechRepublic (May 4, 2000), http://www.techrepublic.com/article/lock-it-down-block-tcp-ip-ports-to-increase-security/.

[17] *Remote Desktop Connection*, PC World (Aug. 17, 2011), http://www.pcworld.com/article/234326/remote_desktop_connection.html.

[18] *Remote-Access VPNs Provide Secure Access*, CISCO, http://www.cisco.com/c/en/us/solutions/enterprise-networs/security/networking_solutions_products_genericcontent0900aecd8051f37b.html; *Virtual Private Networking: An Overview*, Microsoft: Technet (Sept. 4, 2001), https://technet.microsoft.com/en-us/library/bb742566.aspx.

[19] Karen Scarfone & Paul Hoffman, *Guidelines on Firewalls and Firewall Policy*, Nat'l Inst. Standards and Tech. Special Publication 800–41, Rev. 1 (Sept. 2009), https://ws680.nist.gov/publication/get_pdf.cfm?pub_id=901083.

§ 4.04 APPLYING PATCHES: KEEPING YOUR SOFTWARE AS SECURE AND UP-TO-DATE AS POSSIBLE

We have discussed password policies and firewalls as two basic steps to ensure that your court's system will not be the low-hanging fruit that is particularly appealing to hackers. Another important and easy step a court can take to help shore up its defenses is to apply updates and patches in a timely fashion. While it would be unreasonable to insist that a court apply patches as soon as they are released (especially to production servers), statistics on exploited public and private organizations show that administrators generally take far too long to apply patches. Verizon's 2015 Data Breach Investigations Report found that 99.9 percent of private organizations compromised through the exploitation of a known vulnerability had actually been compromised more than a year after the vulnerability was published and publicized.[20] That statistic means that administrators were waiting longer than a year to patch known vulnerabilities. Such a delay is clearly not best practice. Actual best practice depends on the precise nature and risk profile of each public or private organization; but a regular and timely application of patches is essential to maintaining good security hygiene.[21]

The following areas should be considered first and foremost when applying patches:

1. patches to operating systems (Windows, Linux, Mac);
2. patches to firewalls, wireless routers, and other network devices;
3. patches to user applications such as Microsoft Office, Google Chrome, Adobe Acrobat, and Adobe Flash; and
4. recommended configuration changes.

The last item, recommended configuration changes, is as important as the first three but often overlooked. It does not require installing updated files; rather, it is usually centered on changes to a configuration (such as to the Windows registry) or an option in an application. An example is the disabling of older versions of Secure Sockets Layer (SSL) on a web server.[22] SSL deals with encrypted communication between a client and a server. Older versions are vulnerable to some attacks.

---

[20] *2015 Data Breach Investigations Report*, Verizon Enterprise Solutions, http://higherlogicdownload.s3.amazonaws.com/GOVERNANCEPROFESSIONALS/a8892c7c-6297-4149-b9fc-378577d0b150/UploadedImages/Landing%20Page%20Documents/DBIR%20Executive%20Summary%20vv%204-10-15.pdf.

[21] For more information, *see* Daniel Voldal, *A Practical Methodology for Implementing a Patch Management Process*, SANS (2003), https://www.sans.org/reading-room/whitepapers/bestprac/practical-methodology-implementing-patch-management-process-1206; Rick Rosato, *Best Practices for Applying Service Packs, Hotfixes and Security Patches*, Microsoft: Developer Network, https://msdn.microsoft.com/en-us/library/cc750077.aspx.

[22] *What Is SSL (Secure Sockets Layer) and What Are SSL Certificates?*, Digicert, https://www.digicert.com/ssl.htm.

§ 4.05 PERIMETER SECURITY CONTROLS: WHAT IT TAKES TO KEEP THE BAD GUYS OUT

Owners of homes and businesses protect their facilities with locks, guards, alarm systems, and other forms of security. The type of protection may be as simple as a lock on a door; but quite often, it involves multiple layers of security with notifications for various events. Access to gain entry into a facility is controlled by keys, codes, and identification. The more guarded the facility, the more layers are in place. Your court's network can and should be controlled the same way.[23] Protecting your perimeter is an important deterrent to those who wish to gain access to your court's environment.

As discussed previously, one of the most basic protections for your court's perimeter is a firewall, a device that usually sits between the court's network and the outside world. See figure 4-1 for a rendition of a typical network with a firewall.[24]

The diagram in figure 4-1 illustrates the placement of a firewall within a network. It shows two purposes of a firewall: first, connectivity between the Internet and laptops and desktops in the court's environment;[25] and second, connectivity for servers that communicate with the outside world.[26] Be they email, web, or FTP servers, the latter type are collectively known as *forward-facing servers*, in that they are directly accessible by others using the Internet.[27] Note that the email and FTP servers are in a separate area from the rest of the network. Such a placement is commonly known as a "demilitarized zone" (DMZ).[28] Forward-facing servers are placed in a DMZ because they require more open communication with the outside world, and their accessibility from the outside world makes them more likely to be compromised.[29] Should those servers become compromised, the rest of your court's network can be protected by limiting the type of network traffic that occurs between the servers in the DMZ and the rest of the computers in your court's environment.[30]

---

[23] John Edwards, *Security At the Edge: Locking Down the Network Perimeter*, IT SECURITY (Feb. 4, 2008), http://www.itsecurity.com/features/security-edge-020408/.

[24] Margaret Rouse, *Firewall* [definition], TECH TARGET, http://searchsecurity.techtarget.com/definition/firewall.

[25] *Id.*

[26] *Id.*

[27] *See generally Security Best Practices to Protect Internet Facing Web Servers*, MICROSOFT, http://social.technet.microsoft.com/wiki/contents/articles/13974.security-best-practices-to-protect-internet-facing-web-servers.aspx.

[28] Margaret Rouse, *DMZ (demilitarized zone)* [definition], TECH TARGET, http://searchsecurity.techtarget.com/definition/DMZ.

[29] *Id.*

[30] *Id.*

FIGURE 4-1 Typical Network With Firewall

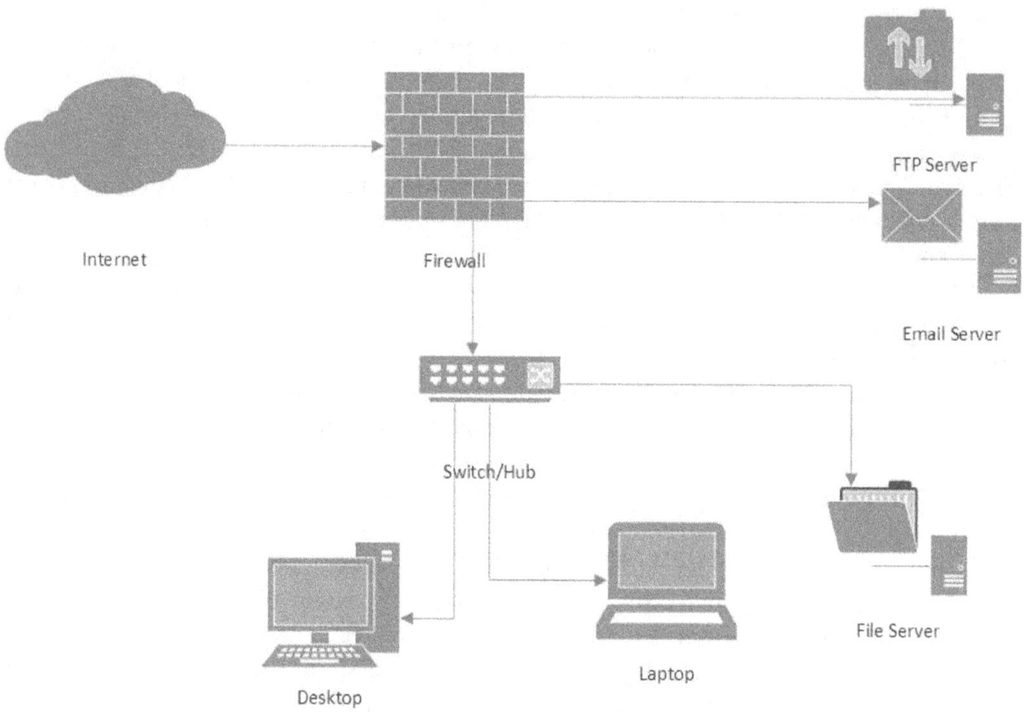

With its placement in your court's environment, the firewall is perfectly set up to be a traffic cop for communications between your network and the Internet.[31] What can that traffic cop do? First, it can limit the communications.[32] For example, your court's email server may also have a built-in web server so that judges and staff can retrieve email via a web browser. A proper way to implement that feature is not to allow traffic over unencrypted HTTP (e.g., http://myemail.com) but rather only over encrypted HTTPS (e.g., https://myemail.com), such that only HTTPS traffic gets to the web server. A properly configured firewall should be set up to enable only the necessary traffic and to deny all other traffic. The other thing that a traffic cop can do is look for inappropriate traffic. What if your court's email server all of a sudden started accepting FTP requests or starting sending traffic to another FTP server? The firewall can be configured to look for such traffic and block it. Another example would be finding unencrypted, readable data being sent over HTTPS, which is an avenue for encrypted communications. Lastly, your court's firewall can also act as a traffic cop by looking for traffic going to or coming from certain IP addresses.[33]

---

[31] Lewis & Knopf, CPAs, PC, *Computer Protection: Call a Traffic Cop* (Mar. 2010), https://www.lewis-knopf.com/uncategorized/computer-protection-call-a-traffic-cop/.

[32] *Id.*

[33] For an example of creating these types of rules, *see Add or Edit Firewall Rule,* MICROSOFT: TECHNET (Feb. 21, 2013), https://technet.microsoft.com/en-us/library/cc753558.aspx.

Another device that can help with protecting a court's perimeter is an intrusion detection system or intrusion protection system (IDS/IPS).[34] An IDS/IPS sits inside your network and monitors traffic for suspicious activity.[35] Think of an IDS/IPS as an antivirus (AV) application, but for network traffic. Your AV is programmed to look for applications with specific signatures or behaviors that indicate they are viruses.[36] An IDS/IPS looks for patterns or behaviors that would indicate someone may have hacked into your court's computer network and is stealing data.[37] It is not a replacement for a firewall, nor is a firewall a replacement for an IDS/IPS. The two devices work in tandem to block traffic and identify malicious traffic.[38]

However, your court's firewall needs somewhere to report just as an alarm system requires a response and your guards have to report incidents to someone. More precisely, your court needs someone to monitor the firewall and other potential security incidents. Monitoring of firewall and similar logs is one of the most neglected security activities. What some organizations with all the protection in the world fail to realize is that if no one is watching what is going on, you cannot properly respond when an incident occurs. Take the previously-mentioned example of blocking certain IP addresses: How does a court know what IP addresses to block? Monitoring a firewall and an intrusion detection system (IDS) can indicate consistent, malicious activity coming from a specific IP address. With that information, the firewall can be configured to block all traffic to and from that address.

Monitoring helps develop a baseline of expected network traffic,[39] and creation of a baseline is paramount to finding malicious activity.[40] The reason public organizations will not monitor correctly or even forgo monitoring altogether is that a firewall or IDS system can generate a daunting amount of data. For large public organizations, it can be downright impossible.[41] The solution is to generate a baseline of expected traffic[42] for the court environment. A baseline will also inform as to how much data will typically traverse the firewall to the outside Internet. With that information, rules can be created to identify

---

[34] Matthew Berge, *What Is Intrusion Detection?* SANS, https://www.sans.org/security-resources/idfaq/what-is-intrusion-detection/1/1; Margaret Rouse, *Intrusion Detection (ID)* [definition], Tech Target, http://searchmidmarketsecurity.techtarget.com/definition/intrusion-detection.

[35] Matthew Berge, *What Is Intrusion Detection?* SANS, https://www.sans.org/security-resources/idfaq/what-is-intrusion-detection/1/1.

[36] Margaret Rouse, *Antivirus Software* [definition], Tech Target, http://searchsecurity.techtarget.com/definition/antivirus-software.

[37] Berge, *supra* note 35.

[38] Joel Snyder, *Do You Need an IDS or IPS, or Both?*, Tech Target, http://searchsecurity.techtarget.com/Do-you-need-an-IDS-or-IPS-or-both.

[39] *Baseline Process Best Practices* (White Paper), CISCO (Oct. 3, 2005), https://www.cisco.com/c/en/us/support/docs/availability/high-availability/15112-HAS-baseline.html.

[40] Vangie Beal, *Intrusion Detection (IDS) and Prevention (IPS) Systems*, Webopedia (July 15, 2005), http://www.webopedia.com/DidYouKnow/Computer_Science/intrusion_detection_prevention.asp.

[41] Richard Bejtlich, *Top Seven Network Traffic Monitoring Challenges*, Tech Target (Apr. 16, 2011), http://searchnetworking.techtarget.com/tip/Top-seven-network-traffic-monitoring-challenges.

[42] *See, e.g.*, Michael Brandenburg, *How to Set a Network Performance Baseline for Network Monitoring*, Tech Target (July 2010), http://searchnetworking.techtarget.com/How-to-set-a-network-performance-baseline-for-network-monitoring.

unusual types of or large increases in network traffic.[43] To illustrate this concept, let us review one private organization's recent experience with a data breach. An investigation revealed that the stolen information had been compressed into ZIP files and the ZIP files renamed as JPG files. The fake JPG files were then put on the organization's public-facing website and downloaded from there. No alarms were triggered, because JPG files being downloaded from a website is quite normal. But if the organization had set a trigger for very large JPG files such as these, then it might have detected and stopped the activity.

One trap that public and private organizations commonly fall into is the "set it and forget it" mindset.[44] Security is an ever-evolving discipline. Formerly good doctrine can become a bad practice. Years ago, for example, it was considered secure to dispose of hard drives by using a magnet to wipe them clean.[45] But only extremely powerful magnets are effective at wiping today's hard drives, so magnetic wiping is no longer considered a best practice.[46] The other issue with "set it and forget it" is that hackers are constantly evolving their methods and attacks.[47] Each time Microsoft, Apple, US-CERT (through the CVE list), or anyone else publishes a new vulnerability, hackers take aim at organizations' networks to exploit it. Especially when the vulnerability has no automated fix or no fix at all, public or private organizations can defend themselves only by adjusting their protections.

Perimeter controls should not end with a firewall or IDS/IPS system. The firewall protects one entry point into your court's network. What other entry points might a court or court system have that need protection? Consider the following list:[48]

1. Mobile devices. Cell phones and tablets are quite often used outside of your network and then connected to your organization's internal network. These devices therefore constitute another entry point on your perimeter. Any perimeter protection plan should include defenses for these devices. Encryption (discussed later) and proper password management (previously discussed) should be considered. But one must also consider limiting the type of data accessible by mobile devices, as well as mobile device management (MDM) tools that allow remote deactivation, locating lost devices, and wiping of stolen devices.

---

[43] *Avoiding Network Traffic Confusion with Consistent Firewall Rules*, Tech Target, http://searchsecurity.techtarget.com/magazineContent/Avoiding-Network-Traffic-Confusion-with-Consistent-Firewall-Rules.

[44] Fred Donovan, *The Days of a "Set It and Forget It" Approach to Endpoint Security Are Over, Says ESG*, Firce IT Security (Jan. 13, 2015), http://www.fierceitsecurity.com/story/days-set-it-and-forget-it-approach-endpoint-security-are-over-says-esg/2015-01-13.

[45] Craig Wright, *Overwriting Hard Drive Data*, SANS (Jan. 15, 2009), https://digital-forensics.sans.org/blog/2009/01/15/overwriting-hard-drive-data/.

[46] *Id.*

[47] *Hackers Are Evolving*, Comms Bus. (Dec. 14, 2015), http://commsbusiness.co.uk/features/hackers-are-evolving/.

[48] For a deeper analysis of new points of entry that affect perimeter security, *see* Axel Buecker et al., *Understanding IT Perimeter Security*, IBM (2008), http://www.redbooks.ibm.com/redpapers/pdfs/redp4397.pdf.

2. Wireless networks. Whether for internal staff or for visitors, wireless networks are another entry point into your environment. Some courts or court systems dispense with wireless networks altogether. Best practices will segment or separate guest networks from the rest of a court's network environment, often with physically separate network cables, switches, routers, and Wi-Fi equipment, to prevent any access to the court's environment through a wireless network. Finally, routine scanning is important in order to identify new wireless networks that may pop up in your court environment. A cell phone or tablet acting as a wireless hot spot, if not monitored, can be a recipe for disaster.
3. Portable storage devices. Tapes, CD/DVDs, and USB drives must all be considered perimeter devices, as they can contain litigant or other stakeholder data and be accessed outside of your court environment. Encryption of these devices is discussed later; but some courts and court systems choose to restrict their use altogether by a technological means.

§ 4.06 ENCRYPTION

Use of encryption technology has become more widespread recently, but it is still underutilized. In encryption, data is put through a formula that codes or "encrypts" it with a key.[49] The key is usually password-protected. The larger the key, the more difficult it becomes to brute-force decrypt the data.[50] The key is usually "pseudo-random generated" through an algorithm built into an encrypting application for which the user creates a pass-phrase.[51] Multiple applications perform encryption, and there are various uses for it. However, two types are basic: symmetric key encryption and public key encryption.

Symmetric key encryption is used in applications such as True Crypt, VeraCrypt, and Microsoft's BitLocker. The data is encrypted and decrypted with the same key.[52] Therefore, judges or court staff who communicate among themselves using symmetric key encryption must both have the same key.

In public key encryption, the data is encrypted with a publicly-shared key[53] but cannot be decrypted with the same key. Instead, it has to be decrypted with a private key, which is held by the recipient of the data. Let us explain this process a little further. Say Organization A and Organization B want to use public key encryption to exchange data. Each organization would provide the other with its public key, allowing each to encrypt data being sent to the other organization. However, if the public key was stolen, the

---

[49] Margaret Rouse, *Encryption* [definition], Tech Target, http://searchsecurity.techtarget.com/definition/encryption.

[50] Margaret Rouse, *Brute Force Cracking* [definition], Tech Target, http://searchsecurity.techtarget.com/definition/brute-force-cracking.

[51] Rouse, *supra* note 49.

[52] Margaret Rouse, *Secret Key Algorithm (Symmetric Algorithm)* [definition], Tech Target, http://searchsecurity.techtarget.com/definition/secret-key-algorithm.

[53] Margaret Rouse, *Asymmetric Cryptography (Public-Key Cryptography)* [definition], Tech Target, http://searchsecurity.techtarget.com/definition/asymmetric-cryptography.

encrypted data would still be safe because decrypting the data requires the private key (which ideally neither organization would share, as neither would need to).

With that definition in mind, let us discuss the various uses of encryption.

The most common use of encryption occurs (though many do not realize it) when one is browsing a secure website denoted by "https" or a secure FTP site denoted by "ftps" at the beginning of the URL. The "s" after "http" or "ftp" signals that the browser and website will use the Secure Sockets Layer (SSL) protocol.[54] SSL uses the public key encryption method just described.[55] When browsing secure websites, however, it is important that your browser reports that the certificate is valid. Websites create or purchase certificates from a small group of certificate authority (CA) organizations.[56] Organizations, particularly courts, should make sure to use SSL whenever possible to prevent various attacks. SSL is commonly used for email access via a website, or on FTP sites for downloading encrypted data. If your court's FTP server does not support "ftps," then your court should consider encrypting the contents of the files being transferred (as discussed later in this chapter).

Encryption is also vitally important for secure email communications. Secure email communication can be done in one of two ways. The first method is to use a provider.[57] The recipient of a secure email communication will get an email that provides a link to log into a website that of course communicates via SSL as described earlier. Once logged in, the recipient can read the secure message and then securely reply to the sender. The second method of secure email communications is to implement public/private key encryption.[58] This form of encryption works by having the two parties exchange their public keys. Each party encrypts its messages using the recipient's public key. The recipient then decrypts the message using its own private key. Many current email solutions facilitate this sharing of keys.

Years ago, full-disk encryption was unpopular as the process was very resource intensive, and encrypted hard drives would thus run more slowly. With today's faster processors, increased memory, and more streamlined encryption processes, omitting encryption of a court's devices is not recommended.[59] Multiple versions of Microsoft Windows come with BitLocker already built in,[60] a full disk encryption scheme that makes use of the Trusted Platform Module (TPM) chip. The TPM chip helps with encryption by, among other things, storing the encryption keys.

---

[54] Margaret Rouse, *Secure Sockets Layer (SSL)* [definition], Tech Target, http://searchsecurity.techtarget.com/definition/Secure-Sockets-Layer-SSL.

[55] *Behind the Scenes of SSL Cryptography*, Digicert, https://www.digicert.com/resources/SSL_Cryptography_Explained.pdf

[56] Margaret Rouse, *Certificate Authority (CA)* [definition], Tech Target, http://searchsecurity.techtarget.com/definition/certificate-authority.

[57] Eric Geier, *How to Encrypt Your Email*, PCWorld (Apr. 25, 2012), http://www.pcworld.com/article/254338/how_to_encrypt_your_email.html.

[58] Margaret Rouse, *Pretty Good Privacy (PGP)* [definition], Tech Target, http://searchsecurity.techtarget.com/definition/Pretty-Good-Privacy.

[59] *Full-Disk Encryption (FDE)*, WhatIs, http://whatis.techtarget.com/definition/full-disk-encryption-FDE.

[60] *See BitLocker Drive Encryption Overview*, Microsoft, https://technet.microsoft.com/en-us/itpro/windows/keep-secure/bitlocker-overview.

Disk encryption should not be restricted to just a court's computers. USB devices for transferring data to others should also be encrypted.[61] Consider that the majority of the documents judges or their staff will exchange with others are likely to be confidential and to contain personally identifiable information (PII) or other sensitive data.[62] Losing a laptop or USB drive not set up with encryption may result in mandatory disclosure of the loss and, for some entities, in fines by government agencies.

You can label documents "confidential" or "judge's eyes only" all you want; but if the drive on which the data is stored gets lost or stolen, it really is not confidential anymore. Encrypting the data is relatively easy, and several popular encryption applications are free and somewhat easy to use. Best practices for using this type of software start with creating an encrypted container on a drive. You can put the application on the unencrypted part of the drive. Your sensitive documents are then put in the encrypted part. Sending data in this fashion allows one to rest easy knowing that if the drive is lost or stolen in transit, the encrypted documents on the drive are safe. The encrypted data is protected by a password, which is usually transmitted via email after the drive reaches its destination. Do not put the password on the drive or on a memo sent with the drive. Doing so defeats the purpose of encrypting the data.

Mobile devices such as cell phones and tablets often have encryption built in.[63] In fact, all new iPhones released in the past few years have automatically encrypted their data.[64] All a user needed to do was implement a PIN for access to the phone, and the encryption protection would be complete. Encryption on Android phones is a simple task that usually takes less than an hour to implement. Because millions of cell phones are stolen yearly and likely contain sensitive data in the form of messages and documents, cell phone encryption is a no-brainer.

One may want to consider encrypting sensitive data on servers in your court's environment. Depending on the type of data and on requirements for retaining that data, encryption may be an option. The chosen protection depends on a court's requirements and on the goals of encryption. If the goal is to prevent access to stolen devices, full-disk encryption will provide that protection.[65] Content on devices that are locked, logged out, or turned off will be inaccessible to anyone who does not have the proper credentials to decrypt the data. But consider a server containing data with various levels of confidentiality: That server is always on and accessible by those with the proper credentials. In such a case, full-disk encryption would not be helpful in protecting the data. But sensitive data such as personnel records or confidential, case-related information could be

---

[61] *Encrypt Your Thumb Drive*, WIRED, https://technet.microsoft.com/en-us/library/ff404223.aspx.

[62] David G. Ries, *Safeguarding Confidential Data: Your Ethical and Legal Obligations*, 36 LAW PRACTICE 4 (July/Aug. 2010), http://www.americanbar.org/publications/law_practice_home/law_practice_archive/lpm_magazine_articles_v36_is4_pg49.html.

[63] Robert Sheldon, *Mobile Data Encryption Techniques: On-Device and On-the-Go*, TECH TARGET, http://searchmobilecomputing.techtarget.com/tip/Mobile-data-encryption-techniques-On-device-and-on-the-go.

[64] Robert Sheldon, *How Apple iOS Encryption and Data Protection Work*, TECH TARGET, http://searchmobilecomputing.techtarget.com/tip/How-iOS-encryption-and-data-protection-work.

[65] *Full-Disk Encryption (FDE)* [definition], WHATIS http://whatis.techtarget.com/definition/full-disk-encryption-FDE.

stored in encrypted databases. Encrypting a database applies an additional level of security. The separation of accounts used to access the server from those used to access the database completes this layer of protection. Then, should a server account become compromised, the hacker will need to compromise an additional account to access the encrypted database.

Most forms of encryption are protected through the use of a password. As discussed previously in this chapter, proper password management is key to maintaining the effectiveness of passwords, and the same holds true here: A court's encrypted data is only as safe as the password chosen to protect that encryption. A password like "password" or "1111" can render the encryption moot. Furthermore, encryption can be made stronger on mobile devices by setting them to wipe or reset themselves after a certain number of invalid attempts ten) (usually 10), rendering any data on the device unrecoverable. Other types of encryption are managed with keys or certificates.[66] In large organizational environments, certificates are generated and used to encrypt network traffic and documents. When certificates or keys are not being used, they should be stored in a secure location. Some types of certificates, called *trusted root certificates*, are used to generate other certificates for encryption, and to authenticate certificates.[67] These trusted root certificates are used only periodically and therefore often stored on encrypted drives, which are then unplugged from the computer and locked in a cabinet. The reason for this added protection is that if the trusted root certificate fell into the wrong person's hands, certificates could be generated to thwart encrypted communications or perform other malicious activities.

The largest benefit of encryption is that many privacy laws consider encrypted data to be inaccessible, so if such data is lost or stolen and a court or court system can prove that it was properly encrypted, usually that court does not have to report the records stolen.[68] Many times, a side-benefit of encrypted data is enforcement of "need to know": Unless I have the key, I cannot see what the data contains, so the risk of someone seeing data they should not see is removed.

§ 4.07 SUMMARY

Many public and private organizations today are hacked not because they were targeted but rather because hackers could easily compromise their systems. The first step to keep your court from being hacked is to avoid being an easy target—the low-hanging fruit. Timely updating of computers, having a proper password policy, and implementing even a basic firewall all go a long way toward making sure your court or court system is not hacked just because it was the easiest target. The next step is creating perimeter controls to protect your court or court system's environment. These controls will not only

---

[66] *See, e.g., Symantec Managed PKI for SSL*, SYMANTEC, https://www.symantec.com/ssl-certificates/managed-pki-ssl/#.

[67] *Manage Trusted Root Certificates*, MICROSOFT: TECHNET, https://technet.microsoft.com/en-us/library/cc754841.aspx.

[68] *Data Breach Disclosure Regulation: Today's Challenge*, THALES E-SECURITY, https://www.thales-esecurity.com/solutions/by-business-issue/data-breach-notification.

make it difficult for a hacker to enter your network but will also allow for monitoring of traffic between your network and the Internet. And encryption can be a very effective tool for protecting a court or court system's sensitive data in the event its perimeter security measures are breached.

CHAPTER 5

CRYPTOGRAPHY

Daniel Garrie, Esq., Judge Leo M. Gordon, Rick Borden, and Jeff Stapleton

§ 5.01 Introduction
- [A] Why Is Cryptography Important Today?
- [B] What Is Cryptography and How Does It Differ From Encryption?

§ 5.02 Encryption

§ 5.03 Message Authentication

§ 5.04 Digital Signatures

§ 5.05 Key Management
- [A] Key Generation
- [B] Key Distribution
- [C] Key Storage
- [D] Key Backup and Recovery
- [E] Key Revocation
- [F] Key Expiration
- [G] Key Termination

§ 5.06 Other Crypto Considerations
- [A] Vendor Selection
- [B] Jurisdictional Law

§ 5.07 Conclusion

Appendix 5-1 Chapter Glossary

§ 5.01 INTRODUCTION

[A] Why Is Cryptography Important Today?

More than ever before, personal, confidential, and other sensitive information is being transmitted over the Internet through emails, shared files, and the cloud, which are all potentially exposed.[1] Many individuals as well as small and large public and private organizations today increasingly rely on technology but do not fully understand the importance of data, software, and systems security.[2] Individuals as well as small public and private organizations typically do not have information security knowledge or cybersecurity expertise. Larger public and private organizations might not have cybersecurity expertise or sufficient funds to manage an information security group properly. Moreover, even security professionals have trouble using programs and tools intended for security purposes.[3] As a result, several private organizations have recently suffered major data breaches resulting in high-profile litigation.[4] Damages can be massive, and additional losses can include: the time and cost of credit monitoring (direct and indirect); years of systemic, obtrusive, organization-wide audits to identify and correct not just the source of the leak but also other broken business processes discovered during the audits;[5] for a court or court system in particular, a long-term impact to its integrity; and data theft as well as destruction of files, servers, and storage systems.[6] A basic knowledge of cryptography, encryption, and cybersecurity is necessary to help users understand how important they are in the network that keeps both their own as well as the court's data safe.

---

[1] "A major catalyst for email encryption were revelations about widespread online surveillance in documents leaked by Edward Snowden, the former National Security Agency contractor." Agence France-Presse, *NSA Spying Inspires ProtonMail End-to-End Encrypted Email Service* (May 19, 2014), http://gadgets.ndtv.com/internet/news/nsa-spying-inspires-protonmail-end-to-end-encrypted-email-service-526769; *see also* Miners, *NSA Sniffing Prompts Yahoo to Encrypt Traffic Between Its Data Centers* (Apr. 3, 2013), http://www.computerworld.com/s/article/9247410/NSA_sniffing_prompts_Yahoo_to_encrypt_traffic_between_its_data_centers.

[2] *See* Garrie, *The BYOD Dilemma: How to Keep Your Assets from Turning into Liabilities* (2014), http://blog.legalsolutions.thomsonreuters.com/wp-content/uploads//2014/02/BYOD-white-paper.pdf.

[3] Sasse & Flechais, *Usable Security: Why Do We Need It? How Do We Get It?*, Security an Usaility: Designing Secure Systems that People can Use 13, 14 (O'Reilly Media, 2005).

[4] Sony, Target, and eBay are among the most recent victims. *See, e.g.*, Ellis, *Lawsuits Say Sony Pictures Should Have Expected Security Breach* (Dec. 20, 2014), http://www.cnn.com/2014/12/20/us/sony-pictures-lawsuits/.

[5] *See* FTC Red Flags Rule (Nov. 9, 2007), http://www.ftc.gov/sites/default/files/documents/federal_register_notices/identity-theft-red-flags-and-address-discrepancies-under-fair-and-accurate-credit-transactions-act/071109redflags.pdf.

[6] The event coordination site Meetup was shut down for seven days by a hack known as a distributed Denial-of-Service attack (DDOS), causing losses in the hundreds of thousands of dollars, in addition to the disruption of communities whose organizers rely on the website. *See* Newman, *Aggressive Hackers Brought Meetup Down. Here's How It Came Back* (Mar. 10, 2014), http://www.slate.com/blogs/future_tense/2014/03/10/ddos_attacks_brought_meetup_down_but_now_it_has_better_network_security.html.

[B] What Is Cryptography and How Does It Differ From Encryption?

The term *cryptology* contains the originally Greek combining forms *crypto-*, meaning "secret," and *-logy* "study," and refers to the discipline of covert communications. The related terms *cryptography* and *cryptanalysis* respectively mean the practice of secret writing and the undoing of secret writing. The earliest known users of cryptography were the Egyptian priesthood circa 1900 B.C., who substituted their own secret symbols for hieroglyphics. Ancient cryptography such as the Caesar cipher and pre-modern cryptography such as the Playfair cipher were manually computed by individuals. Modern cryptography, ushered in by World War II, is too complex for simple paper-and-pencil calculations and requires the processing power of computers.

We can think about cryptography as a specialized branch of mathematics that offers various information security controls, including data confidentiality (encryption), data integrity and authentication (message authentication), and the possibility of nonrepudiation (digital signatures). The term *encryption* is commonly misused as an equivalent of cryptography, but this is a misnomer that can lead to invalid assumptions analogous to calling every fastener a "nail" when actually nails, screws, staples, cement, tape, and glue are all used in building a house. If the architect, general contractor, bricklayer, plumber, electrician, dry-waller, and other construction workers called everything a nail, there would be mass confusion and many mistakes. Different types of cryptographic functions provide different security controls and are sometimes used in combination, so correct naming can get complicated. Let us first provide a few definitions to be used throughout this chapter.

Cryptographic algorithms are processes of discrete steps performed by a computer to transform data, with inputs consisting of the data to be transformed, associated processing parameters which might include a *cryptographic key*, and the transformed data as output. Note that some algorithms do not use keys, whereas others may use one or more. Algorithms exist in mathematics, computer science, and many other disciplines; however, a cryptographic algorithm has more rigor and (it is hoped) fewer bugs and design flaws.

Cryptographic protocols are the ways people implement one or more cryptographic algorithms to establish cryptographic keys or exchange data securely by sending messages over an unsecured environment (e.g., the Internet). Let us consider a simple protocol example with two people, Alice and Bob, in which Alice wants to send data (here, a series of questions) to Bob, who will answer. Alice wants some assurance that the eventual answer will be from Bob and not from someone else—for example, Eve. So Alice and Bob decide to exchange a secret number, seven to be included in one form or another in the data as a way to show the data was from Alice to Bob or vice versa. They agree to set up a protocol: Any time Alice sends data to Bob, she includes a number she chooses at random. When Bob responds with the answer, he includes the product of Alice's random number and their secret number, seven. Their messages might look like this:

Alice's Question	*Bob's Answer*
5: Who won the 1965 World Series?	35: Los Angeles Dodgers
3: Who won the 1973 Super Bowl?	21: Miami Dolphins
2: Who was the drowsy dwarf?	15: Slugo

Alice sends the random numbers 5, 3, and 2 and verifies Bob's answers 35 and 21, because 5 x 7 = 35 and 3 x 7 = 21. However, because 7 x 2 = 14 ≠ 15, Alice can detect that the third message may not be from Bob (and thus the drowsy dwarf might not be Slugo). This simple protocol does not actually prove anything; it only indicates that the first two answers likely came from Bob and the third likely did not. Bob may have miscalculated the third answer due to a programming error. Eve may have stolen the secret number, coerced Bob, or determined (using cryptanalysis) that the secret number was seven. After all, how hard can it be to factor the product of two prime numbers? The lesson here is that, just like algorithms, protocols can have bugs. They might be too transparent. Or their security can be compromised if the participants (Alice and Bob) do not follow the rules.

Cryptographic keys are strings of binary zeros and ones used with cryptographic algorithms. Keys control how the algorithm transforms input data into output data. Different keys will yield different outputs for the same input, as will different inputs using the same key. Depending on the algorithm, keys may be a random number for use with *symmetric cryptography* or a mathematically-generated number for use with *asymmetric cryptography*. Generally speaking, keys must only be used by authorized entities; they must be kept secret unless someone actually needs to know them (and we will see a valid exception to this for public key cryptography); and they cannot be used indefinitely but rather go through a lifecycle and must be changed periodically. The lesson here is that keys must be managed properly—hence the term *key management*. Our next brief discussion of symmetric and asymmetric cryptography will be followed in more depth by the application of each in encryption.

Symmetric cryptography algorithms use the same key to perform both a function and the function's inverse. Anyone with access to the symmetric key can execute the function or its inverse and transform data accordingly. Thus, it is imperative that only authorized individuals have access to the symmetric keys. Note that certain algorithms, sometimes called one-way functions, have no inverse function. Symmetric keys are often called *secret keys* to distinguish them from asymmetric keys.

Asymmetric cryptography algorithms use two different but mathematically-related keys: One is used to perform a function, the other to perform the inverse function. Further, one key can be made public while the other is kept private. The public key cannot be used to determine the private key, such that it can be shared with many others. (Here is the exception to key secrecy mentioned earlier.) Hence, we get the term *public key cryptography*. Unlike symmetric cryptography, public key cryptography allows anyone to access the public key without endangering the corresponding private key; only the authorized individual needs access to the private key.

Cryptography has primarily been a tool for soldiers, ambassadors, and spies to convey important information covertly. Military couriers would send orders to the battle front or return tactical battlefield situations to headquarters. Ambassadors might have received political instructions or returned important economic information. And spies, of course, would send critical information about . . . spy stuff. Encryption would have kept an adversary from reading the information in any intercepted messages; but sometimes learning that a secret message had been sent might have been as important as the message's content.

Two aspects must be considered when we think about protecting information: data in transit and data in storage. *Data in transit* happens when information is transmitted over the Internet from one location to another (Alice to Bob) using mobile devices, laptop or desktop computers, network appliances, midrange servers, or even mainframes. Data transmission includes file transfers, emails, text messages, videos, voice messages, and even old-fashioned telephone calls. These transmissions might originate over cellular, Bluetooth, near field communications (NFC), Wi-Fi, or local area network (LAN) connections. *Data in storage* happens when information is temporarily or permanently stored. For example, the sender (Alice) and receiver (Bob) both often store data on their respective local devices; but many intermediate systems across networks and across the Internet temporarily store the data in passing. Let us consider the various threats that can be deterred using cryptography.

- *Data disclosure* happens when an unauthorized individual (Eve) gets copies of personal information by mistake or accident from the legitimate sender or receiver, or from a bad actor who intentionally stole data from the sender, receiver, or an intermediary system on the Internet.
- *Data modification* happens when an individual (Eve) changes or replaces personal information by mistake or accident on the sender, receiver, or intermediary system; or when a bad actor intentionally changes data on the sender, receiver, or an intermediary system.
- *Entity masquerading* happens when a bad actor (Eve) intentionally sends, receives, or falsifies information on an intermediary system so that it appears to be from a legitimate source.

Each of these threats is answered by different cryptographic algorithms and protocols that can provide various security controls: data confidentiality, data integrity, and data authentication. Data confidentiality can be achieved through *data encryption*, preventing disclosure of data in transit or in storage. Data integrity can be achieved through *message authentication*, enabling detection of modified data in transit or in storage. *Digital signatures* can provide both data integrity and entity authentication, avoiding entity masquerading. Cryptography can also provide the technological foundation for *nonrepudiation*[7] (as described later in this chapter), but such services raise additional legal considerations.

Symmetric cryptography cannot provide nonrepudiation, because anyone with legitimate access might use the keys, making it impossible to prove data integrity and

[7] J. J. Stapleton, Nonrepudiation, *in* Security Without Obscurity: A Guide to Confidentiality, Authentication, and Integrity (CRC Press, 2014).

authentication independently to a third party. But asymmetric cryptography can provide nonrepudiation, because only a legitimate user can access the private key. Further, the Digital Signature Guideline (DSG)[8] published by the American Bar Association's Information Security Committee essentially describes the requirements for a nonrepudiation service by which a sender and receiver may protect each other from false claims:

> Signer authentication and document authentication are tools used to exclude impersonators and forgers and are essential ingredients of what is often called a non-repudiation service in the terminology of the information security profession. A non-repudiation service provides assurance of the origin or delivery of data in order to protect the sender against false denial by the recipient that the data has been received, or to protect the recipient against false denial by the sender that the data has been sent. Thus, a non-repudiation service provides evidence to prevent a person from unilaterally modifying or terminating legal obligations arising out of a transaction effected by computer-based means.

Another quasi-cryptography subject is *electronic signatures*, which should not be confused with digital signatures. (Digital signatures are described in more detail later in this chapter.) The Uniform Electronic Transactions Act (UETA) defines an electronic signature as an electronic sound, symbol, or process attached to or logically associated with a contract or other record and executed or adopted by a person with the intent to sign the record. The UETA definition is consistent with the European Union (EU) Directive on Electronic Signatures.

§ 5.02 ENCRYPTION

Encryption is the transformation of readable data by normal means into indecipherable data, thus providing data confidentiality. *Decryption* is the inverse function, or transformation of the indecipherable data back into the original readable format. Encryption algorithms have clear-text (or plaintext) data as input and ciphertext as output. Decryption algorithms have cipher-text as input and clear-text data as output. For example, a sender (Alice) might encrypt a clear-text message into ciphertext and transmit the ciphertext to a recipient (Bob); then the receiver (Bob) can decrypt the cipher-text back into the original clear-text message. As another example, a user can encrypt a clear-text note into ciphertext, store the ciphertext onto a device, and then later retrieve the ciphertext from the device and decrypt the ciphertext back into the original clear-text note. Figure 5-1 and figure 5-2 illustrate the overall processes.

[8] Information Security Committee (ISC), Electronic Commerce and Information Technology Division, Section of Science and Technology, & American Bar Association (ABA), Digital Signature Guidelines: Legal Infrastructure for Certification Authorities and Secure Electronic Commerce (Aug. 1996).

FIGURE 5-1: Symmetric Encryption

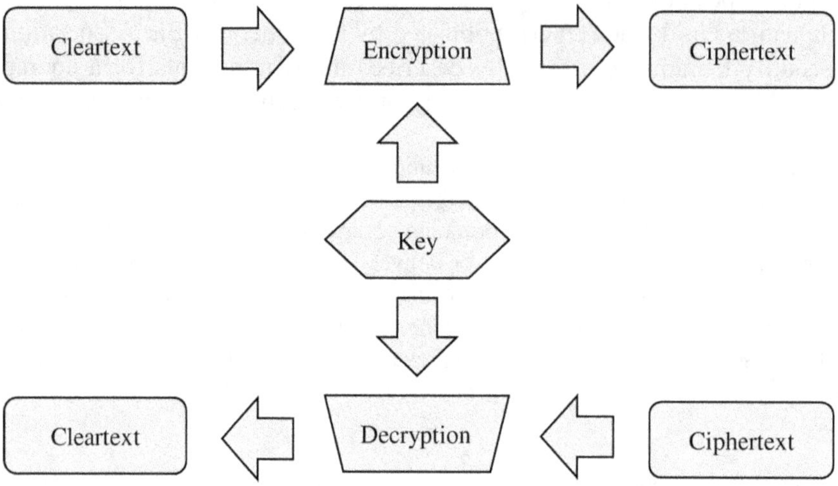

The encryption process actually has two inputs (the clear-text and a cryptographic key); its inverse function, decryption, likewise has two inputs (the ciphertext and the same key). When the same key is used for both encryption and decryption, it is called *symmetric encryption* (shown in figure 5-1); in contrast, when two different, mathematically-related keys are used, it is called *asymmetric encryption* (shown in figure 5-2). However, symmetric and asymmetric encryption are not used interchangeably, and asymmetric encryption is not the same technique as *digital signatures* (discussed in § 5.04 of this chapter). These two points are often misunderstood, which can lead to invalid assumptions or a bad security analysis, so some discussion is worthwhile.

FIGURE 5-2: Asymmetric Encryption

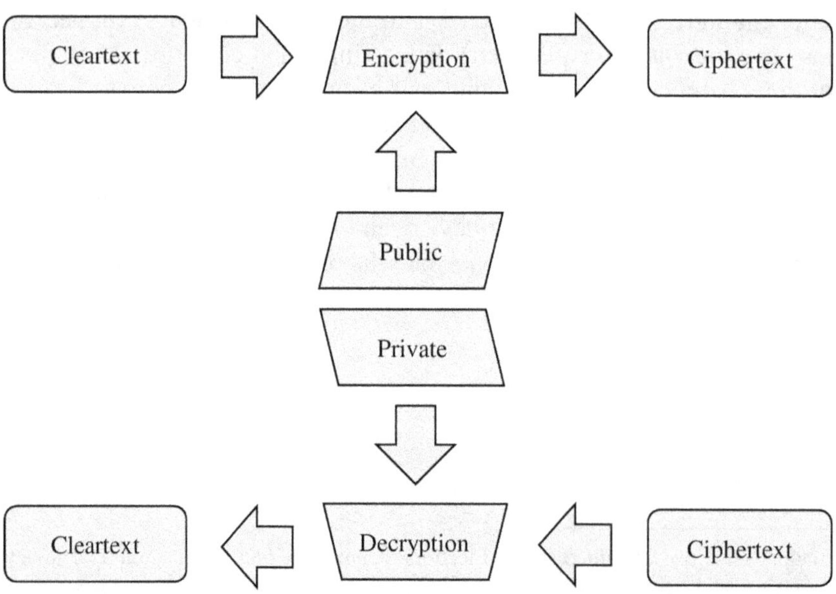

Without delving too deeply into the mathematics of asymmetric cryptography, suffice it to say that asymmetric encryption has limitations that symmetric encryption does not have. First, clear-text gets encrypted using the public key in asymmetric encryption, which anyone might have; but ciphertext gets decrypted using the private key, which only the owner has. Second, asymmetric encryption works best with small bits of clear-text, whereas symmetric encryption works with small bits, medium messages, and large files. Third—and perhaps more importantly—asymmetric cryptography consumes more computing power than symmetric cryptography. Thus, symmetric cryptography is faster, requires little memory, and takes up very little disk storage. The differences are significant enough that symmetric cryptography is used to protect data far more often than asymmetric cryptography. In fact, asymmetric encryption is so resource-costly that it is typically used to protect symmetric encryption keys rather than data (as discussed in § 5.05 on key management). Meanwhile, we have yet to explore the risks of symmetric encryption.

§ 5.03 MESSAGE AUTHENTICATION

Message authentication is the use of symmetric cryptography to detect data modification and provide limited entity authentication. Unlike encryption, which can prevent data disclosure, message authentication can only detect a problem; it cannot prevent an attacker from changing or replacing information. Cryptography is used to create a message authentication code (MAC) which can later be reused to verify that the data has not been attacked. *Verification* is the inverse function of the original MAC generation and recreates the MAC for comparison. Figure 5-3 illustrates the overall process.

Similar to encryption, the MAC generation function has two inputs (the clear-text and a symmetric key); however, the output differs such that a MAC is produced. Unlike decryption, the MAC verification function has the clear-text and the key as inputs; the output is a recalculation of the MAC, such that the original MAC is compared to the recomputed MAC to determine if the clear-text has been changed. For example, Alice generates the MAC and sends both it and the clear-text to Bob. Bob then recalculates the MAC using the received clear-text, and compares the newly-recomputed MAC to the received MAC. If either the clear-text or the MAC has been changed during transmission, Bob's MAC will not match Alice's MAC. Unfortunately, Bob only knows the verification has failed; he does not know what actually happened.

FIGURE 5-3: Message Authentication

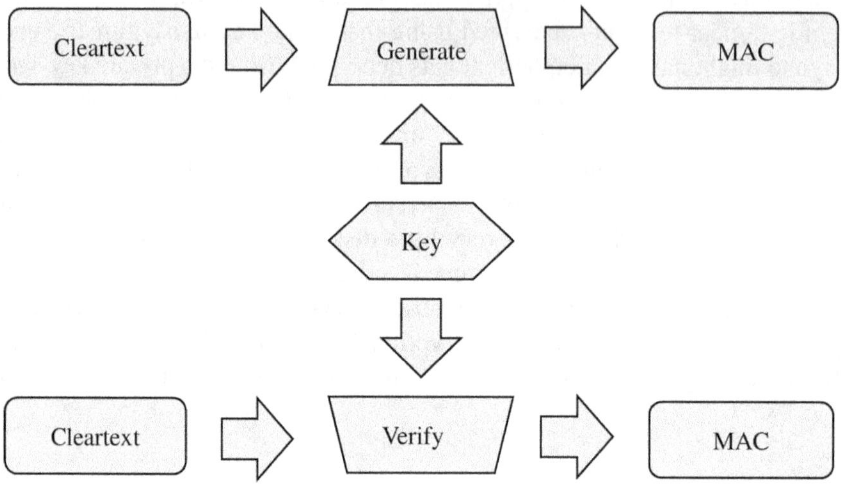

Conversely, if the MAC does verify, then Bob knows two things. First, he knows the clear-text has data integrity, that is, his version of the clear-text is the same as what Alice sent. Second, he can authenticate Alice, because only he and Alice have access to the symmetric MAC key, and Bob knows he did not send the clear-text to himself (he can rule out other senders). However, if the symmetric MAC key has been shared with anyone else, the entity authentication cannot be definitive. Also, even if the symmetric MAC key is only accessible to Alice and Bob, the entity authentication is not provable to a third party, so the message does not have nonrepudiation. Any crypto-savvy third party (perhaps, a judge) would realize that Bob could have falsified the clear-text, because the verification function calculates the MAC just like the generation function, using a shared symmetric key.

§ 5.04 DIGITAL SIGNATURES

A *digital signature* uses asymmetric cryptography to detect data modification and provide entity authentication. Unlike asymmetric encryption, digital signatures are generated using the private key and verified using the corresponding public key. And unlike message authentication, the private key is only accessible to the signer, whereas any verifier can have a copy of the public key. When we discuss digital signatures, the preferred (and technically correct) terms are *sign the data* (clear-text) and *verify the signature.* Other terms or phrases, commonly misused, include e*ncryption*, *encrypt* and *decrypt* the *hash*, and *sign the hash.*

FIGURE 5-4: Digital Signatures

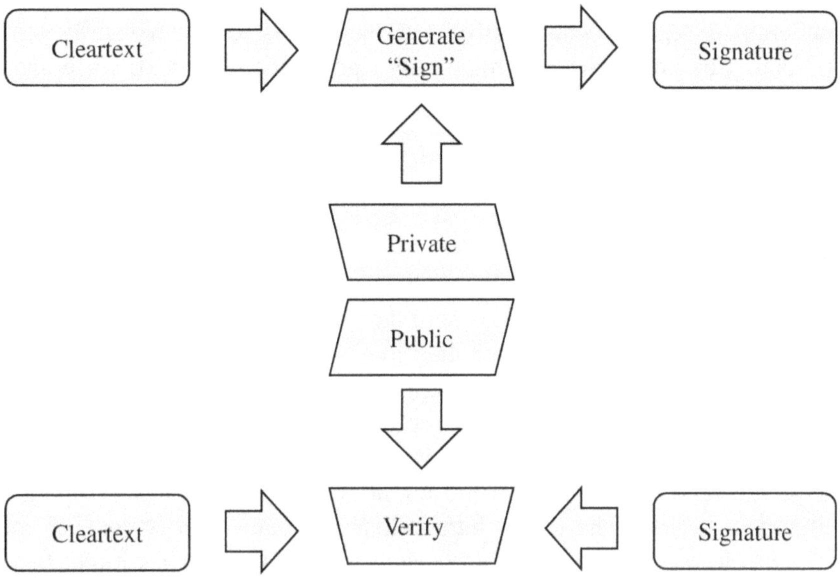

Perhaps one of the reasons for the bad terminology or loose usage is that the first commercially-used asymmetric algorithm for digital signatures was RSA,[9] named for its inventors Rivest, Shamir, and Adleman. It just so happens that RSA is reversible—that is, it can encrypt with the public or the private key and, inversely, decrypt with the private or public key. Ironically, few digital-signature algorithms have this property. Instead, most *sign* using the private key but can only *verify* using the public key. Strict use of the terms *sign the data* and *verify the signature* sidesteps the need to think about the underlying cryptography and thus avoids bad assumptions.

Another point of confusion: Digital signatures always include a hash algorithm. None is shown in figure 5-4 simply because the hashing function is part of the signature generation and verification processes. The clear-text is always hashed before the private key is used to create, as well as before the public key is used to verify, the signature. This is true for all digital signature algorithms, such that the hash algorithm can be considered as just part of the overall cryptographic process. Basically, we know the hash is there; and for most discussions, it can simply be taken for granted.

With digital signatures, similar to message authentication, one party signs the data and another party verifies the signature. For example, Alice generates a signature using her private key and sends it and the clear-text to Bob. Bob then verifies the signature using Alice's public key. If either the clear-text or signature has been changed during transmission, the verification will fail, but Bob only knows it failed; he does not know what actually happened. Most important to realize is that Bob has nothing but Alice's public key, and Alice can provide her public key to dozens or thousands of individuals without endangering her private key.

---

[9] Rivest, Shamir, & Adleman, *A Method for Obtaining Digital Signatures and Public-Key Cryptosystems,* COMMUNICATIONS OF THE ACM, 120–26 (Feb. 1978).

Conversely, if the digital signature does verify, Bob knows three things. First, he knows the clear-text has *data integrity*—that his version is the same Alice sent. Second, he can authenticate Alice, because only Alice has access to her private key. Third and most importantly, he knows Alice cannot deny signing the clear-text, since again, she is the only one with access to the private key. Because (allegedly) only Alice has access to the private key, integrity and authentication are provable to a third party, which gives us a foundation for *nonrepudiation*.

§ 5.05 KEY MANAGEMENT

Both symmetric and asymmetric keys all have a common management lifecycle[10] as shown in figure 5-5. Basically only the timeframes differ, depending on how keys are utilized. The lifecycle stages (generation, distribution, storage, backup and recovery, revocation, expiration, and termination) always occur in a specific order; but not all stages are always needed. In general, unless security controls are in place for each lifecycle stage, any key is susceptible to being compromised, affecting encryption, message authentication, or digital signatures. The lesson here is that adequate security controls must be in place for each stage of the lifecycle; but because some of the stages might be under the control of different individuals, groups, or even applications, interoperability, as well as cooperation among the various participants, is essential.

FIGURE 5-5: Key Management Lifecycle

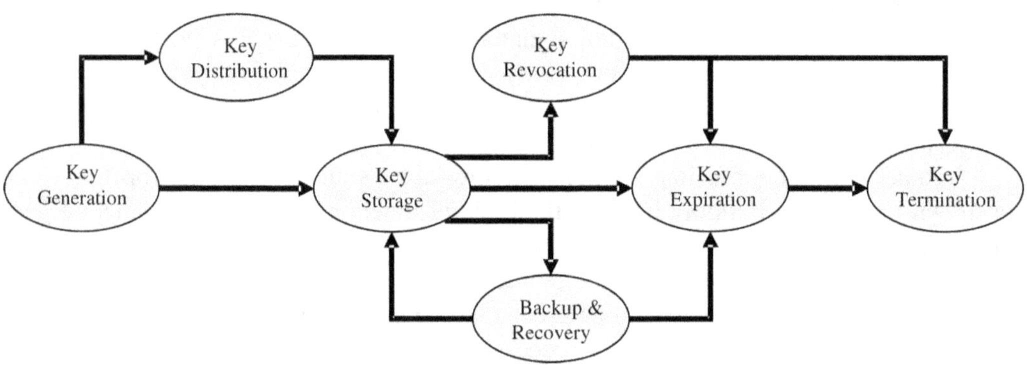

[A] Key Generation

Key generation happens when symmetric keys are randomly generated, or when asymmetric private and public key pairs are mathematically computed. When asymmetric keys are generated, the process includes obtaining a public key certificate from an

[10] AMERICAN NATIONAL STANDARD X9.79 PUBLIC KEY INFRASTRUCTURES (PKI), Part 4: Asymmetric Key Management, aligns numerous International Organization for Standardization (ISO), Accredited Standards Committee (ASC X9), and National Institute of Standards and Technology (NIST) key management lifecycle models.

organization called a certificate authority (CA), part of an overall public key infrastructure[11] (PKI). The role of the CA is to authenticate the requestor (Alice) and issue a certificate that can be trusted by a relying party (Bob). A basic certificate contains many data fields, including the key-pair-owner's name (Alice) and her public key, the name of the issuing CA, the CA's digital signature (the CA thus also has its own asymmetric key pair), and a certificate validity date.

[B] Key Distribution

Key distribution occurs when two or more participants must share one or more keys. For example, if Alice generates an encryption key, then she needs to establish the key with Bob. Or, if Bob generates a message authentication key, he needs to exchange the key with Alice. In both examples, symmetric keys need to be securely distributed between Alice and Bob so that Eve cannot intercept the keys. For digital signatures, Alice must share her public key certificate with Bob but does not need to worry about Eve.

Alice might transmit keys to Bob (*key transport*), or Alice and Bob might use cryptographic methods to derive them mutually (*key agreement*); the preferred generic term to address either method is *key establishment*. Alternatively, when a key is generated, stored, and used at the same location (such as for file encryption), key distribution might not be needed. Thus, the lifecycle for some keys might jump from generation directly to storage, thereby skipping distribution.

[C] Key Storage

Key storage happens after generation or distribution when keys are being used for their intended purposes, such as for encryption, message authentication, or digital signatures. The keys must be protected from disclosure, modification, replacement, and unauthorized access. Controls must also be implemented so that keys are only used for their intended purposes and cannot be accidentally or intentionally misused. Furthermore, keys cannot be used forever—they all expire, upon which their use ends. Coordinating key change among multiple participants can be challenging.

For example, when Alice and Bob change their encryption key, some messages might be processed out of order, such that the old and new keys are both active: Alice encrypts and sends ten messages, the first five with the old and the next five with the new key. Bob might then receive or process the messages in a different order, without knowing which key to use for decryption. If Bob uses the incorrect key, decryption will result in invalid clear-text, and depending on the nature of the clear-text and the processing rules, it might result in a message or application error. Worse, the error might go undetected and cause a processing error. Such key synchronization errors are often difficult to detect or diagnose.

---

[11] J. J. Stapleton & W. Clay Epstein, Security without Obscurity: A Guide to PKI Operations (CRC Press, 2016).

Access controls to protect cryptographic keys vary based on the product. The strongest method is to use specialized cryptographic hardware that never allows a clear-text key outside its security boundary and performs the cryptographic algorithms and protocols inside its cryptographic boundary. Another method, using cryptographic software, requires an end-user to enter a password to generate the cryptographic key dynamically so that it is never stored on disk but appears only in computer memory. An even weaker method, also using software, stores the key in a system file protected with mere password-based access controls. Whatever the method, once keys are securely stored with appropriate access controls and used in accordance with their purpose, the next stages have to be considered: backup and recovery, revocation, and expiration.

[D] Key Backup and Recovery

If an operational outage due to a disabled key is unacceptable, one might need to implement key backup and recovery. Copies of keys can be stored safely, such that in the unlikely event of an application failure corrupting or erasing them, they can be restored in a timely manner during the application recovery process. For example, if Alice's message authentication key fails because her computer crashes, she can restore the key after her computer is replaced. Thus, she can recover it and continue exchanging messages with Bob.

But keys need not always be recovered—and in some cases, it is better when they cannot be. For example, if Alice's private key for digital signatures fails, she could recover it and continue to sign messages for Bob to verify using her public-key certificate. However, the backup copy of Alice's private key poses an unacceptable risk, because if it was ever compromised, then Eve could generate counterfeit signatures. Thus, if Alice's computer crashes, it would be better for her to generate a new key pair and provide Bob with a new certificate.

Conversely, the certificate authority (CA) that issued Alice's public-key certificate would back up its private certificate-signing key. From an operational perspective, the CA might have issued thousands of certificates relied on by millions of parties, so it would be better for the CA to keep using the same private key rather than generate new keys and then have to redistribute its own certificate to those millions of relying parties.

[E] Key Revocation

Key revocation might be needed before a key expires to prevent its use. Because revoked keys should not be used, applications need a method to validate their status. Further, revoked keys have an expiration date like any other key. Thus if a certificate revocation list (CRL) is used to track revoked certificates, then once a certificate expires per its validity date, it no longer has to be kept on the CRL. This is true for all keys: Revoked or expired keys should not be used, and backed-up, revoked, or expired keys should not be restored.

There are many operational and security reasons to revoke keys. From a security perspective, for example, a key should be revoked if it is known or suspected to be compromised. From an operational perspective, the key should be revoked to avoid its misuse if an application is decommissioned. When an employee departs or is dismissed, or when an individual dies, that person's key should likewise be revoked. Revocation is typically associated with expiring certificates, but in fact any key can and, in such cases, should be revoked. Another control against accidental use of revoked keys is to *terminate* the key.

[F] Key Expiration

Key expiration marks the end of a key's useful lifetime. For example, Alice should not encrypt data using an expired key, though Bob might need one to decrypt previously encrypted data. Likewise, Alice should not use an expired message-authentication key, but Bob might need to verify a previously generated MAC. Thus, the same symmetric key can expire in different time frames depending on its cryptographic versus its inverse function. Similarly, Alice should not sign messages using her private key when the corresponding public key has expired per its certificate validity date, while Bob might need to use an expired certificate to verify an older signature. (Knowing when a message has been signed is therefore extremely important.) Once expired keys lack any valid use, they can then be properly *terminated* to avoid anyone misusing or reusing them.

[G] Key Termination

Key termination is the process of systematically destroying all copies of expired keys to prevent reuse or recovery. To accomplish this, symmetric keys must be deleted. Asymmetric private keys must be deleted when certificates are revoked. Public-key certificates are typically not deleted, because without the corresponding private key, the public key is relatively benign. There might also be hundreds or thousands of certificate copies at unknown locations, so deleting them all is not realistic. Key termination includes all types of media, including stored files, printed paper, and peripherals such as smartcards and USB memory-sticks. Practically speaking, a key inventory is needed so that terminated keys can be tracked.

§ 5.06 OTHER CRYPTO CONSIDERATIONS

[A] Vendor Selection

The fundamental problem with purchasing cryptography solutions is that an organization cannot buy what does not exist. Unless an organization is crypto-savvy, willing to acquire patent licenses, and then to design, develop, and maintain its own custom solutions, there is always a worrisome dependency on commercially available products. Granted, this is true for most technologies; but as this chapter has pointed out, proper use of cryptography and secure management of cryptographic keys raises numerous concerns. A court or court system might blissfully trust its vendor, hoping the vendor knows far more than the court staff about cryptography, key management, business processes, and application environments. Because the court or court system understands far better than anyone else its own operational processes, governing statutes, court rules, and application environment, it needs to determine its own security requirements and educate itself about cryptography and key management.

Courts or court systems need to stipulate their security requirements, evaluate products based on relevant criteria, and determine the product(s) that fit best. Because vendors must serve many clients across different sectors, they cannot afford to build custom solutions. Rather, vendors often rely on sector security standards to determine requirements. Therefore, it is in a court or court system's own self-interest to influence standards so that vendors will build products it can rely upon. Claims of compliance with standards must also be validated. The mantra here is: *Verify, then trust.* Unfortunately, many standards bodies have no compliance programs, so although the standards are worthwhile, a product's conformity with them is not easily measured. The lesson is to understand your security requirements and recognize that today, while cryptography is an essential ingredient in any product, it is not the only ingredient. For example, an encryption product that provides good cryptographic algorithms and protocols with secure key-management processes is one thing. But it still has to have well-defined roles and responsibilities with an appropriate separation of duties—including different access controls for end-users, application administrators, system administrators, key court managers, and judicial officers. Thus, a court or court system must establish its cryptographic evaluation criteria before selecting a vendor's product.

[B] Jurisdictional Law

Remarks like "It's a small world" and "The digital age is making it smaller every day" imply that cryptography is a universal language that lets everyone just get along. But this is not actually the case: Many foreign and international jurisdictions have different laws and regulations when it comes to allowing cryptography. For example, in U.S. history before the turn of the Millennium, cryptography was listed as auxiliary military equipment the importation and exportation of which was controlled by the U.S. Department of State. During the 2000s, control over nonmilitary exports was shifted to the U.S. Department of Commerce with restrictions imposed by the Office of Foreign Assets Control (OFAC). Legal issues must be considered when cryptographic products cross jurisdictional boundaries, whether for personal use, general use, or resale, and occasionally when encrypted data crosses borders. Some algorithms are restricted, some key-sizes are limited, and sometimes keys are required to be escrowed. This relates to data recovery: When data is encrypted (ciphertext), it is considered unreadable unless the key for decryption is accessible. Access to the key thus becomes a control factor. But key escrow is not necessarily the answer as the goal is to obtain the data, not necessarily the key. For example, if Alice encrypts data using a key she shares with Bob, an authorized third party might need to read the data. Alice's employer might need to ensure that she is not exposing sensitive data to Bob; or perhaps law enforcement is investigating Bob and needs to see the clear-text. It is invalid to assume that the third party needs access to the key shared by Alice and Bob when in fact it only needs access to the clear-text. Such access can be achieved in various ways:

- A copy of the clear-text could be escrowed before Alice performs the encryption or after Bob performs the decryption.
- Alice might separately encrypt the data, using two different keys: one for Bob and another for the third party.
- Alice might encrypt the data using a key she shares with a proxy service, and the proxy service would decrypt and re-encrypt the data using a key shared with Bob.

Thus, it is unnecessary to impose encryption restrictions. Key-management methods are available to provide data escrow (and not necessarily key escrow) to satisfy third-party access requirements.

§ 5.07 CONCLUSION

For symmetric cryptography to work, sender (Alice) and receiver (Bob) need to use the same cryptographic key, so the problems to be solved are how the users should store, share, and generate the key. With encryption, if the key is compromised—that is, if an unauthorized individual (Eve) gets access to the symmetric key—then copies of the ciphertext can be decrypted. Alice and Bob may think their messages are safe while Eve, knowing or having access to the key, can decrypt ciphertext copied from the Internet. Alarmingly, Eve might collect encrypted messages between Alice and Bob for weeks, months, or years in hopes of getting the key. With message authentication, if the MAC key is compromised—that is, if an unauthorized individual (Eve) gets access to the symmetric key—then messages can be modified. Bob would think a given message is from Alice because the MAC verifies, and cannot detect that Eve, using their compromised key, has changed it and replaced the legitimate MAC with her own. Thus, a compromised key negates both data integrity and entity authentication.

Eve might also be able to intercept the symmetric key at the moment Alice and Bob exchange it. Because they must use the same key, Alice and Bob need somehow to establish the symmetric key securely, such that Eve cannot capture it. There are many good ways to exchange keys securely, including manual processes, the use of separate key-encryption keys (KEKs) to exchange symmetric data-encryption keys, and the use of asymmetric keys to establish symmetric encryption keys. And conversely, there are also many bad ways to exchange keys. The best practice is to use products and follow procedures that comply with industrial security standards such as those published by the International Organization for Standardization (ISO[12]), the American National Standards Institute (ANSI[13]), the Accredited Standards Committee X9 for the financial services industry (ASC X9[14]), and the National Institute for Standards and Technology (NIST[15]).

---

[12] *Available at* www.iso.org.

[13] *Available at* www.ansi.org.

[14] *Available at* www.x9.org.

[15] *Available at* www.nist.org.

For asymmetric cryptography to work, sender Alice needs to protect her private key, and receiver Bob needs to validate Alice's certificate. If Alice's private key is not securely stored, Eve might make a copy without Alice's knowledge. If access to Alice's private key is not controlled, Eve might not have to steal it but rather simply guess the password to access it. Either way, such access would let Eve generate a digital signature that Bob would verify and that a third party would presume to be valid. Further, if Bob ever challenged Alice over a digital signature, Alice might claim Eve had compromised her private key (whether it actually happened or not) and deny ever signing the clear-text. Again, digital signatures can only provide the technical foundation for nonrepudiation services; implementing nonrepudiation requires further controls.

Information security controls (confidentiality, integrity, authentication, and nonrepudiation) provided by cryptography (encryption, message authentication, digital signatures, and key management) are part of a larger picture: cybersecurity. Cyber threats are on the rise worldwide as business and government leaders declare them a major priority.[16] The field of cryptography is vast, and this chapter has only been able to touch on the surface concepts. But that does not lessen the importance of security for all users of the Internet and mobile devices. Best practice in crypto-cybersecurity is constantly evolving as the give-and-take continues between hackers and network defense systems, so it is important to stay updated and informed. Many excellent guides to Internet security and encryption exist with more detail and examples than we are able to provide here. Gaining even some knowledge, however slight, of the systems that come into play every time you hit "send" on an email or download a file can only be beneficial, and we hope that this chapter may encourage you to do further research in the field.

APPENDIX 5-1

Chapter Glossary

Asymmetric cryptography—Algorithms that use two different but mathematically related keys; one key is used to perform a function, and the other key is used for the inverse function.

Cryptographic algorithms—Processes performed by a computer to transform data, with inputs (data and parameters) and output (the transformed data).

Cryptographic key—Used with a cryptographic algorithm, a string of binary zeros and ones that controls how the algorithm transforms input data into output data.

Cryptographic protocols—Implementation of one or more cryptographic algorithms to establish cryptographic keys or exchange data securely over an unsecured environment.

Cryptography—A specialized branch of mathematics that offers data confidentiality (encryption), data integrity and authentication (message authentication), and nonrepudiation (digital signatures).

[16] *See, e.g.*, Garrie, *Cybersecurity Becoming Real Issue for Boards of Directors*, Daily J. (Jun. 2, 2014); Barlyn, *Wall Street Watchdog to Bolster Reviews of Brokerage Security*, Reuters (Oct. 29, 2014), http://www.reuters.com/article/2014/10/29/us-finra-cybersecurity-examinations-idUSKBN0II2DA20141029.

Data encryption—Transformation of readable data (clear-text) into indecipherable data (ciphertext), thus providing data confidentiality.

Digital signature—Asymmetric cryptography used to detect data modification and provide entity authentication.

Key management—Secure supervision of cryptographic keys throughout their lifecycle.

Message authentication—Symmetric cryptography used to detect data modification and provide limited entity authentication.

Public key cryptography—Asymmetric cryptography wherein public keys are distributed as digital certificates and used for digital signature verification, data encryption, or key management schemes; and wherein the corresponding private keys are used for digital signature generation, data decryption, or key management.

Symmetric cryptography—Algorithms that use the same key to perform both a function and its inverse.

CHAPTER 6

ISO STANDARDS

Daniel Garrie, Esq. and Judge Leo M. Gordon

§ 6.01 Introduction
[A] Overview of the ISO

§ 6.02 ISO Standard 27001
[A] Establishing Security Objectives
[1] Data Confidentiality
[2] Data Integrity
[3] Data Availability
[B] Identifying Security Needs
[C] Implementing a Security Program
[D] Ensuring Compliance

§ 6.03 ISO Scope and Certification
[A] Auditing an Organization's Compliance
[B] Scope of an ISMS
[C] ISO Standard 27001's Statement of Applicability

§ 6.04 Conclusion

§ 6.01 INTRODUCTION

It is indisputable that in today's world of widespread cyberattacks, courts and court systems must establish effective cybersecurity procedures and practices. While there is no definitive best standard, a leading option is the ISO 27000-series standards promulgated by the International Organization for Standardization (ISO).

In this chapter we will be examining three standards in the series: standard 27000:2018, *Information technology—Security techniques—Information security management systems—Overview and vocabulary*; standard 27001:2013, *Information technology—Security techniques—Information security management systems—Requirements*,[1] and standard 27002:2013, *Information technology—Security techniques—Code of practice for information security controls.*[2]

Courts and court systems may look to these information security management standards in order to secure both their own as well as their stakeholders' data[3] and litigation-related information.[4] Adopting security-management standards enhances trust in courts and court systems and promotes confidence in the rule of law throughout society.[5]

[A] Overview of the ISO

The ISO, which comprises 162 national standards bodies, develops "voluntary, consensus-based, market relevant International Standards that support innovation and provide solutions to global challenges."[6] It was founded in 1946 and promulgated its first standard in 1951.[7] The ISO has developed more than 19,000 international standards in fields ranging "from technology, to food safety, to agriculture and healthcare."[8] The ISO has also been integral in developing standards for information security management. These standards are often used as the basis for an accreditation performed by independent, neutral third-party auditor.[9]

---

[1] ISO/IEC 27001:2013, http://www.iso.org/iso/home/store/catalogue_tc/catalogue_detail.htm?csnumber=54534.

[2] ISO/IEC 27002:2013, http://www.iso.org/iso/home/store/catalogue_tc/catalogue_detail.htm?csnumber=54533.

[3] *Safe and Secure: Cyber Security Practices for Law Firms*, CAN Professional Counsel, https://www.cna.com/web/wcm/connect/61aec549-ac28-457b-8626-aa791c782459/Safe_Secure_Cyber_Security_Practices.pdf?MOD=AJPERES.

[4] Mary Pratt, *Law Firm Makes a Case for Security Certification,* CIO (Aug. 28, 2015), http://www.cio.com/article/2969323/security/law-firm-makes-a-case-for-security-certification.html.

[5] *Id.*

[6] *About ISO*, ISO, http://www.iso.org/iso/about.htm.

[7] *Id.*

[8] *Id.*

[9] For a more thorough examination of the certification (accreditation) process, see § 6.03, *infra.*

The ISO 27000-series standards play a pivotal role in offering broad guidance to public and private organizations alike as to how they should deal with information security issues in a comprehensive and methodical way.[10] Additionally, ISO standard 27001's focus on risk assessment allows the standard to be implemented to "keep pace with changes to the security threats, vulnerabilities and [operational] impacts" of an organization.[11] This ensures that organizations that implement the standard can always work to address new threats as time goes on. That said, these standards do not explicitly dictate which steps an organization must take in order to secure its information systems; rather, organizations "are free to choose whichever specific information security controls are applicable to their particular information security situations, drawing on those listed in the standards and potentially supplementing them with other *a la carte* options (sometimes known as extended control sets)."[12]

§ 6.02 ISO STANDARD 27001

ISO standard 27001 defines its scope as outlining "the requirements for establishing, implementing, maintaining and continually improving an information security management system within the context of the organization. [ISO standard 27001] also includes requirements for the assessment and treatment of information security risks tailored to the needs of the organization."[13] This section explores key elements of ISO standard 27001 and considers how courts and court systems can use it to develop and implement cybersecurity regimens that should provide a good deal of protection and shelter them from liability in the event of a data breach.[14] The goal of the standard is for an organization to be able to: (1) establish security objectives; (2) identify security needs; (3) implement a security program; and (4) ensure compliance.[15]

[A] Establishing Security Objectives

The goal of implementing an information security measure is to protect one of the following: (1) data confidentiality,[16] (2) data integrity,[17] or (3) data

[10] Dejan Kosutic, *What Is Cybersecurity and How Can ISO 27001 Help?* 27001 Academy (Oct. 25, 2015), http://advisera.com/27001academy/blog/2011/10/25/what-is-cybersecurity-and-how-can-iso-27001-help/.

[11] ISO/IEC 27001, IsecT, http://www.iso27001security.com/html/27001.html.

[12] *Id.*

[13] ISO/IEC 27001:2013, § 1.

[14] Nell Gluckman, *To Satisfy Clients, Law Firms Submit to Cybersecurity Scrutiny*, Am Law Daily (Mar. 12, 2015), http://www.americanlawyer.com/id=1202720468020/To-Satisfy-Clients-Law-Firms-Submit-to-Cybersecurity-Scrutiny-?slreturn=20160028023722.

[15] David Bodenheimer & Cheryl Falvey, *Cybersecurity Standards and Risk Assessments for Law Offices: Weighing the Security Risks and Safeguarding Against Cyber Threats*, Crowell Moring, https://www.crowell.com/files/Cybersecurity-Standards-and-Risk-Assessments-for-Law-Offices.pdf.

[16] *Confidentiality* is defined in 44 U.S.C. § 3542(b)(1) as "preserving authorized restrictions on access and disclosure, including means for protecting personal privacy and proprietary information."

[17] *Integrity* is defined in 44 U.S.C. § 3542(b)(1) as "guarding against improper information modification or destruction, and includes ensuring information nonrepudiation and authenticity."

availability.[18] Information security professionals often refer to these three goals as the *CIA triad*.[19] Each is discussed in this subsection.

[1] Data Confidentiality

Achieving data confidentiality means that unauthorized people do not access sensitive data. The only way to achieve it is to restrict access to data.[20] The challenge for information security professionals is how to restrict the unauthorized while still allowing the right people access to the data, because such restriction can implicate data availability (discussed later).

One of the first steps that a court or court system should take in establishing its security objectives is to classify its confidential data to ensure the correct balance of protection and transparency.[21] A common data classification breakdown is as follows:

(1) restricted data,[22] (2) private data,[23] and (3) public data.[24] Although care should be taken with all confidential data, this stratification allows proportionate measures to be put into place for each category.[25]

[2] Data Integrity

Maintaining data integrity involves "maintaining the consistency, accuracy, and trustworthiness of data over its entire life cycle."[26] When a court or court system can ensure the integrity of its data, it can be sure that the data has been accessed and modified only by those who are authorized to do so.[27] It is an essential element of the ability to be confident in one's data. From a court's perspective, judges, court managers, court staff, litigants, and their lawyers have a need to know that all of the data they surround themselves with is both accurate and trustworthy. Imagine if every deadline on a court's docket were to be shifted back a week. It might take some time to discover this simple alteration, but

---

[18] *Availability* is defined in 44 U.S.C. § 3542(b)(1) as "ensuring timely and reliable access to and use of information."

[19] Jim Breithaupt & Mark Merkow, *Information Security Principles of Success*, PEARSON (Jul. 4, 2014), http://www.pearsonitcertification.com/articles/article.aspx?p=2218577&seqNum=3.

[20] *Confidentiality, Integrity, and Availability (CIA Triad)* [definition], TECH TARGET: WHATIS, http://whatis.techtarget.com/definition/Confidentiality-integrity-and-availability-CIA (hereinafter "*CIA Triad*").

[21] *Guidelines for Data Classification*, CARNEGIE MELLON UNIVERSITY, http://www.cmu.edu/iso/ governance/guidelines/data-classification.html.

[22] "Data should be classified as Restricted when the unauthorized disclosure, alteration or destruction of that data could cause a significant level of risk to [an organization]." *Id.*

[23] "Data should be classified as Private when the unauthorized disclosure, alteration or destruction of that data could result in a moderate level of risk to [an organization]." *Id.*

[24] "Data should be classified as Public when the unauthorized disclosure, alteration or destruction of that data would results [sic] in little or no risk to [an organization]." *Id.*

[25] Chris Rodgers, *Data Classification: Why is it important for Information Security?* SECURESTATE (Apr. 3, 2012), https://www.securestate.com/blog/2012/04/03/data-classification-why-is-it-important-for-information-security.

[26] *CIA Triad,* supra note 21.

[27] *Integrity* [definition], TECHTARGET, http://searchdatacenter.techtarget.com/definition/integrity.

irreparable harm may have been wreaked on both the court and the litigants in the interim.

A court or court system seeking to protect the integrity of its data must pursue two primary avenues. The first is to implement a system for monitoring potential breaches and, whenever possible, correcting any data that is imperiled by that breach. The second is to implement a rigorous security regimen that will prevent breaches to the greatest possible extent.[28]

[3] Data Availability

In addition to ensuring the confidentiality and integrity of its data, a court or court system must be able to keep that data available. Data availability is ensured by "rigorously maintaining all hardware, performing hardware repairs immediately when needed, and maintaining a correctly functioning operating system environment that is free of software conflicts."[29] In addition to maintaining hardware and software, a central tenet of data availability is that redundancy is necessary to overcome even catastrophic disasters. Redundancy can take many forms from failover,[30] to RAID,[31] to maintaining an offsite backup of critical data.[32] An important consideration in choosing offsite backup is how readily that data can be accessed in the event of a disaster. Take for example a hurricane that knocked out power in New York: If a court had its data backed up to a center in Kansas, the same hurricane could prevent staff from going there to access the data and thus render irrelevant an otherwise effective redundancy.

Getting redundancy in place is necessary to ensure uninterrupted access to a court or court system's data. But courts or court systems often have to choose among redundancy measures and can only choose well if they understand the types of threats to their data. Bad actors have already learned that public organizations rely heavily on readily accessible data and are particularly vulnerable to this threat—and they have begun to attack them by targeting data accessibility.[33] When the international hacking collective

---

[28] Vince Farhat et al., *Cyber Attacks: Prevention and Proactive Responses*, Practical Law Company (2011), https://www.hklaw.com/files/Publication/bd9553c5-284f-4175-87d2-849aa07920d3/Presentation/PublicationAttachment/1880b6d6-eae2-4b57-8a97-9f4fb1f58b36/CyberAttacksPreventionandProactiveResponses.pdf.

[29] *CIA Triad, supra* note 21.

[30] "Failover is a backup operational mode in which the functions of a system component (such as a processor, server, network, or database, for example) are assumed by secondary system components when the primary component becomes unavailable through either failure or scheduled down time." *Failover* [definition], Tech Target, http://searchstorage.techtarget.com/definition/failover.

[31] "RAID (redundant array of independent disks; originally redundant array of inexpensive disks) provides a way of storing the same data in different places (thus, redundantly) on multiple hard disks." *RAID* [definition], TechTarget, http://searchstorage.techtarget.com/definition/RAID.

[32] *CIA Triad, supra* note 21.

[33] Martha Neil, *Unaware "Anonymous" Existed Until Friday, Partner of Hacked Law Firm Is Now Fielding FBI Phone Calls*, ABA Journal (Feb. 6, 2012), http://www.abajournal.com/mobile/article/ unaware_that_anonymous_hacking_group_existed_until_friday_law_firm_partner/; *see also* Scott Shane, *F.B.I. Admits Hacker Group's Eavesdropping*, N. Y. Times (Feb. 3, 2012), http://www.nytimes.com/2012/02/04/us/fbi-admits-hacker-groups-eavesdropping.html?_r=0 (law firm web site defaced and then taken down).

Anonymous launched an attack against a law firm that left its web-host's servers "wiped clean of all client email," the firm was rendered entirely unable to represent its clients effectively during the downtime.[34] A similarly affected court could easily become temporarily useless to litigants waiting for their day in court.

Threats to public organizations can range from improper maintenance causing unreliable server performance, to natural disasters (e.g., fire) destroying the primary data locations, to malicious activities such as distributed denial-of-service (DDOS) attacks[35] preventing access to the data.

[B] Identifying Security Needs

To identify the security needs of a court or court system, a thorough dissection of its existing information technology and security systems is necessary. The goals of this dissection are threefold: (1) Ascertain what data is to be protected, (2) Identify threats to that data, and (3) Forecast the consequences if an attack on that data were to succeed.

ISO standard 27001 can be of great service in identifying and achieving these goals.[36] Other procedures for identifying data assets can be as simple as interviewing the various employees who control information technology systems at different points in the lifecycle of a piece of data.[37] An early, thorough interview can help immensely in determining the idiosyncrasies of a court or court system. Knowing the idiosyncrasies makes the remaining steps far easier.

Once a court or court system's data assets are clearly identified, it is then necessary to classify the data to better understand what security requirements will be needed.[38] This is an important step for a public organization to take because

> [b]y classifying data, a court can prepare generally to identify the risk and impact of an incident based upon what type of data is involved. The classifications- . . . give a basis for determining the impact based upon the level and type of access to data. Together, data classification and level of access drive the operational impact which will determine the response, escalation and notifications of incidents.[39]

---

[34] Scott Shane, *F.B.I. Admits Hacker Group's Eavesdropping*, N. Y. Times (Feb. 3, 2012), http://www.nytimes.com/2012/02/04/us/fbi-admits-hacker-groups-eavesdropping.html?_r=0.

[35] "A distributed denial-of-service (DDoS) attack is one in which a multitude of compromised systems attack a single target, thereby causing denial of service for users of the targeted system. The flood of incoming messages to the target system essentially forces it to shut down, thereby denying service to the system to legitimate users." Margaret Rouse, *Distributed Denial-of-Service Attack (DDoS)* [definition], TechTarget, http://searchsecurity.techtarget.com/definition/distributed-denial-of-service-attack.

[36] ISO/IEC 27001:2013, § 4.2.1.

[37] *Every Company Needs to Have a Security Program,* Applied Trust, https://www.appliedtrust.com/resources/security/every-company-needs-to-have-a-security-program.

[38] Chris Rodgers, *Data Classification: Why Is It Important for Information Security?*, SecureState (Apr. 3, 2012), https://www.securestate.com/blog/2012/04/03/data-classification-why-is-it-important-for-information-security.

[39] *Id.*

The ability to determine this information allows a court or court system to consider the types of threats each class of data may be exposed to. It is important to recognize the countless forms of threats to data, ranging from active attacks[40] to passive attacks[41] or even accidental threats.[42] Such an understanding lets the court or court system properly identify the steps it must take to develop meaningful information security procedures and practices.

Once a court or court system has properly identified and classified its data as well as any threats to it, the organization must begin to analyze the risks associated with those threats. Specifically, it must analyze the potential impact of each recognized threat.[43] This step is critical because it essentially allows the organization to combine the previous steps into a single metric: *risk*. A court can understand its risk only after it understands its data assets, the potential threats, and the harms that may materialize as a result of those threats actually occurring.

The final concern a court or court system must consider as it identifies its security needs are steps to mitigate the potential harm from an actual occurrence.[44] Such mitigation can be either technical or procedural; or in the case of small-impact threats, there can be a conscious decision to accept the harm and take no action. These choices require careful consideration by the court or court system, but once its decisions are reached, it will have a comprehensive identification of all of its security needs.

[C] Implementing a Security Program

Once a court has identified the relevant risks and chosen appropriate mitigation options, the next step is to implement an information security management system (ISMS).[45] ISO standard 27001 is the 27000-series standard that governs the implementation of an ISMS. Due to the breadth of its applicability, ISO standard 27001 does not give explicit instructions on implementing an ISMS but rather "includes suggestions for documentation, internal audits, continual improvement, and corrective and preventive action."[46] A court that chooses to adopt ISO standard 27001 is free to choose whichever specific information security controls apply to its information security situation. It can

---

[40] *Active Attack* [definition], Tech Target: WhatIs, http://whatis.techtarget.com/definition/active-attack.

[41] *Passive Attack*, Tech Target: WhatIs, http://whatis.techtarget.com/definition/passive-attack.

[42] Scott Cole, *Accidental Insider Threats and Four Ways to Prevent Them,* Tech Target, http://searchsecurity.techtarget.com/tip/Accidental-insider-threats-and-four-ways-to-prevent-them.

[43] Proceedings of the Seventh International Network Conference (INC 2008).

[44] *Id.*

[45] "An information security management system (ISMS) is a set of policies and procedures for systematically managing an organization's sensitive data. The goal of an ISMS is to minimize risk and ensure business continuity by pro-actively limiting the impact of a security breach." *Information Security Management System (ISMS)* [definition], TechTarget, http://searchsecurity.techtarget.in/definition/information-security-management-system-ISMS.

[46] *Id.*

draw on those listed in the standard's appendix[47] and potentially supplement them with other *à la carte* options (sometimes known as *extended control sets*).[48]

Implementing an ISMS requires the implementation of training and awareness programs for both personnel and management regarding the ISMS.[49] Untrained personnel often pose the greatest risk to a court's information security systems.

There is a well-established three-step process for training employees: (1) Define which knowledge and skills are required; (2) Conduct trainings to get them to the desired level of knowledge and skill; and (3) Measure whether each individual has achieved the desired level of knowledge and skill.[50] The first step follows directly from the security needs identified earlier, and the third requires regular contact and employee oversight. But the second step, employee training, is the crucial one.[51] Many resources can be utilized to train employees, from having them attend formal courses[52] to disseminating literature or even hiring training consultants.[53] In addition to formal training, it is very important for a court to raise its staff's general awareness of the ISMS it is busy implementing.[54]

[D] Ensuring Compliance

ISO standard 27001 also lays out a framework for monitoring and improving a court's security practices throughout the life of an ISMS.[55] The framework is quite extensive; but at minimum, a court should follow several distinct practices in order to ensure its compliance with the ISMS properly: (1) Execute monitoring and reviewing procedures; (2) Regularly review the effectiveness of the ISMS; (3) Continually re-evaluate the risk; (4) Perform periodic audits; and (5) Continually strive for improvement.[56]

The procedures for monitoring and review should be tailored to detect errors in processing and identify security breaches quickly, and to allow judicial leadership and court management to gauge the effectiveness of controls and of reactions to security incidents.[57] Furthermore, in reviewing these processes, a court should take into account the objectives of the security program, assess whether or not the selected controls are

---

[47] ISO/IEC 27001:2013, Annex A.

[48] ISO/IEC 27001, IsecT, http://www.iso27001security.com/html/27001.html.

[49] Dejan Kosutic, *How to Perform Training & Awareness for ISO 27001 and ISO 22301*, 27001 Axademy, May 19, 2014, http://advisera.com/27001academy/blog/2014/05/19/how-to-perform-training-awareness-for-iso-27001-and-iso-22301/.

[50] *Id.*

[51] *Id.*

[52] *See, e.g., Information Security Training Courses ISO/IEC 27001*, BSI, http://www.bsigroup.com/en-US/ISO-IEC-27001-Information-Security/Training-courses-for-ISO-27001/.

[53] *See, e.g., ISO Consultancy*, http://www.itgovernance.co.uk/iso27001_consultancy.aspx.

[54] Kosutic, *supra* note 52.

[55] ISO 27001, § 4.2.3.

[56] ISO 27001, § 4.2.4.

[57] Rhand Leal, *How to Perform Monitoring and Measurement in ISO 27001,* 27001Academy (June 8, 2015), http://advisera.com/27001academy/blog/2015/06/08/how-to-perform-monitoring-and-measurement-in-iso-27001/.

appropriate and effective, and consider any feedback received from the various stakeholders.[58]

As a court monitors possible threats, it should also review risk assessments at regular intervals as well as after any major organizational or operational changes.

In sum, ISO standard 27001 directs organizations to seek to improve their information security processes and procedures continually. To that end, it directs organizations to regularly implement identified improvements in the ISMS, communicate these improvements to all stakeholders, and ensure that improvements are geared toward the stated objectives of the ISMS.[59]

§ 6.03 ISO SCOPE AND CERTIFICATION

[A] Auditing an Organization's Compliance

Auditing does not help a court plan and implement an ISMS but rather is intended to verify that the court is compliant with the standards; and independent auditors help courts develop their procedures pursuant to them.[60,61] Choosing an independent auditor is a very important decision, but one that only becomes relevant after a court has developed and implemented its ISMS.

[B] Scope of an ISMS

Compliance with ISO standard 27001, however, does not provide the full picture of a court's information security management practices. The scope of compliance allows a court or court system to define what data it will protect at a given time.[62] It is one of the most critical elements in the entire process, because it defines what is subject to the ISMS—and this can vary greatly. For example, a court or court system can be fully compliant with ISO standard 27001 only for a small portion of its information technology systems, which limits the applicability of the ISMS.[63] The scope of an ISMS is considered so critically important that a document outlining the scope of the ISMS is a mandatory requirement for compliance.[64]

---

[58] *Id.*

[59] *Stages of the Development of International Standards*, ISO, https://web.archive.org/web/ 20071005165948/http://www.iso.org/iso/standards_development/processes_and_procedures/stages_description.htm.

[60] *Id.*

[61] *Information Security Management System (ISMS)* [definition], TechTarget, http://search s ecurity.techtarget.in/definition/information-security-management-system-ISMS.

[62] Dejan Kosutic, *How to Define the ISMS Scope*, Advisera 27001 Academy, http://advisera.com/27001academy/knowledgebase/how-to-define-the-isms-scope/.

[63] *Id.*

[64] See § 6.02[C].

ISO standard 27001 compliance is meant for the whole enterprise.[65] But section 4.3 allows a court or court system to define its own scope for an ISMS in each of its units.[66] This flexibility enables the court organization to do a phased implementation of its ISMS—often a more feasible option for it than a single, organization-wide implementation, which can be cost-prohibitive.[67]

[C] ISO Standard 27001's Statement of Applicability

In addition to the scope of ISO compliance, a court or court system must prepare a *Statement of Applicability*, another mandatory requirement under section 6 of ISO standard 27001.[68] While there is no explicit definition, the term "refers to the output from the information security risk assessments and, in particular, the decisions around treating those risks."[69] This means that a court or court system must specify which security measures it intends to use and in what ways those measures will be implemented.[70] Often, organizations use a matrix to match identified risks with the security measures that will be used to address them.[71] The matrix generally uses ISO standard 27002 as a guide for identifying risk controls, but any consistent framework suffices to achieve the goal.

The scope of compliance and statement of applicability are critical elements of a court or court system's ISMS. These documents help an organization to contextualize and understand its ISO standard 27001 compliance and to get a broader sense of its information security practices and circumstances.[72] They enable the court organization to provide clear assurances to others that its system can keep their data secure, and that they can comfortably rely on it.

---

[65] *Id.*

[66] *Id.*

[67] *Planning For and Implementing ISO 27001*, 4 Isaca (2011), http://www.isaca.org/Journal/archives/2011/Volume-4/Pages/Planning-for-and-Implementing-ISO27001.aspx.

[68] *See* ISO 27001, § 6.1.

[69] *Id.*

[70] Dejan Kosutic, *The Importance of Statement of Applicability for ISO 27001*, Advisera 27001Academy, http://advisera.com/27001academy/knowledgebase/the-importance-of-statement-of-applicability-for-iso-27001/.

[71] *Id.* ("The information security control objectives and controls from [ISO 27002] are provided as a checklist at Annex A in order to avoid 'overlooking necessary controls'"). Organizations may use a different framework, such as NIST SP800-55, the ISF standard, BMIS and/or COBIT, or a custom approach. See *supra* Chapter 4.

[72] Kosutic, *supra* note 73:

> If an organization's ISO/IEC 27001 scope only notes "Acme Ltd. Department X", for example, the associated certificate says absolutely nothing about the state of information security in "Acme Ltd. Department Y" or indeed "Acme Ltd." as a whole. Similarly, if for some reason management decides to accept malware risks without implementing conventional antivirus controls, the certification auditors may well challenge such a bold assertion but, *provided* the associated analyses and decisions were sound, that alone would not be justification to refuse to certify the organization since antivirus controls are not in fact mandatory.

§ 6.04 CONCLUSION

ISO standards, particularly ISO standard 27001, can be a great resource for courts or court systems taking steps to secure their information security systems. As lawyers and litigants begin to focus on the security of their data, courts and court systems will need to look toward widely-accepted standards, such as ISO standard 27001, in order to convince these stakeholders as well as the public that their organization can protect the data entrusted to it.

CHAPTER 7

DEFENDING AGAINST THREATS THROUGH INFORMATION SHARING

Daniel Garrie, Esq., Judge Leo M. Gordon, Diana Burley, Cindy Donaldson, and Bill Nelson

§ 7.01 Legal Services: A Big Target for Hackers

§ 7.02 Attacks Are Getting More Frequent and More Sophisticated

§ 7.03 There Is Hope: Courts and Court Systems Should Prepare and Share

§ 7.04 The Legal Services Information Sharing and Analysis Organization

Not too long ago, defending a bank's assets meant adding a rider with a shotgun to the stagecoach or closing the door and spinning the dial on a Mosler bank vault. But over the past few decades, as banking has gone digital, banks have had to evolve their cyber defenses rapidly to mitigate the risk of attacks in the virtual world. Courts and court systems also handle valuable assets and are trusted with equally important data and intellectual property on behalf of litigants. Therefore, courts and court systems need to embrace new approaches to combat evolving threats. This includes courts actively sharing information on threats and vulnerabilities within their own community.[1]

§ 7.01 LEGAL SERVICES: A BIG TARGET FOR HACKERS

As described throughout this book, courts and court systems carry many types of sensitive data that they are obligated to protect. Sensitive data that court and court systems may handle include:[2]

- information about pending mergers and acquisitions or securities data;
- information subject to attorney-client privilege;
- intellectual property and business intelligence;
- corporate documents containing business information on finances, employees, or pending deals;
- information related to criminal actions;
- personally identifiable information (PII) such as social security numbers, personal health information (PHI), and credit card holder data; and
- information relating to bids and appeals on government contracts.

Today's cybercriminals, hacktivists, and even nation-state entities have learned that courts and court systems are a veritable gold mine of valuable information that can be used for a variety of nefarious purposes from espionage to theft, ransom, and harming reputations.

§ 7.02 ATTACKS ARE GETTING MORE FREQUENT AND MORE SOPHISTICATED

Unfortunately, the sophistication and frequency of attacks is increasing. There are numerous tactics that malicious cyber actors use to target institutions. The following are some of the types of threats that courts and court systems face:[3]

- targeted spear-phishing campaigns and "whaling" campaigns, which are spear-phishing campaigns targeting judges and top court executives;

[1] Failure to safeguard information is a violation of the Rules of Professional Conduct and may violate privacy laws such as the Personal Information Protection and Electronic Documents Act, a Canadian federal statute.

[2] See chapter 1.

[3] See chpater 2.

- ransomware attacks, which use malware that restricts access to a computer or system and demands that a ransom be paid to restore access;
- distributed denial-of-service (DDOS) attacks, which can impair critical services on networks or computer systems;
- destructive malware attacks, which destroy data or can even cause physical damage to computer hardware;
- insider threats, including "social engineering" attacks that deceive judges or court staff into revealing sensitive information; and
- increased, purposeful use of disinformation campaigns to sway information services that rely on crowd-sourced data—Google Maps, Waze, and other similar applications—in order to change, restrict or otherwise alter online activity information.

§ 7.03 THERE IS HOPE: COURTS AND COURT SYSTEMS SHOULD PREPARE AND SHARE

Performing risk assessments, developing risk prevention plans, and implementing incident response plans are all critical to defending against cyber threats. But another key aspect of cybersecurity that can benefit all members of the judiciary sector is *information sharing*. Information sharing is part of a community defense strategy whereby multiple courts and court systems share cyber threat information to improve their knowledge of threats to the judiciary collectively and to prepare for them better. Courts can determine ahead of time what sensitive information to share regarding cyber threats, physical threats, and mitigation strategies, and when and how to share it. By pooling their collective data, expertise, and wisdom, individual courts and court systems each contribute to the security and well-being of the judiciary as a whole. Information sharing can result in improved decision making, avoid redundant efforts, and promote alignment with the most up-to-date best practices. In the private sector, this type of sharing is usually facilitated by an information sharing entity called an information sharing and analysis center (ISAC) or information sharing and analysis organization (ISAO). ISACs are generally tied to critical infrastructure sectors as defined in Presidential Decision Directive 63 (PDD 63). ISAOs are industry-specific and enable member organizations to share information properly and effectively within a community in response to the latest threats and vulnerabilities.[4]

§ 7.04 THE LEGAL SERVICES INFORMATION SHARING AND ANALYSIS ORGANIZATION

Courts and court systems can look to the Legal Services Information Sharing and Analysis Organization (LS-ISAO) to see how law firms are addressing cyber threats and vulnerabilities on a sector-wide basis.

[4] Exec. Order No. 13,691 (Feb. 13, 2015). Retrieved from https://www.whitehouse.gov/the-press-office/2015/02/13/executive-order-promoting-private-sector-cybersecurity-information-shari. In fact, the Department of Homeland Security is actively assisting ISAOs and ISACs through a strengthened cyber information sharing program. See https://www.dhs.gov/ciscp.

The LS-ISAO was launched in August, 2015. Many eligible law firms began participating immediately and in fact started sharing information about cyber threats and vulnerabilities. The LS-ISAO is a member-driven organization and has created a trusted community among eligible law firms while building upon existing security-focused practices in the legal industry.

Part of why the LS-ISAO has been able to get up-and-running so quickly is that it chose to partner with the Financial Services Information Sharing and Analysis Center (FS-ISAC). The FS-ISAC was formed in 1999 and is known as one of the most mature information sharing organizations. As of this writing, it serves 7,000 members around the world. The FS-ISAC has been praised as "a key resource on cyber threats for the financial sector and has built a high level of trust over the years."[5] The FS-ISAC is a 501(c)(6) nonprofit organization funded entirely by its member firms and sponsors.

The FS-ISAC serves as an independent, trusted third party that facilitates sharing of actionable information about threats, vulnerabilities, and incidents among its members, the financial services sector, and industry and government partners. It does so in a non-attributable, trusted manner. In its 2014 strategic plan, the FS-ISAC incorporated the objective of assisting other sectors, both to support the "greater good" of information sharing and to do it across sectors where desired.

To let the legal sector focus on improving its defenses rather than operating an ISAO, the LS-ISAO is leveraging the experience and infrastructure that the FS-ISAC has established. This collaboration enables the LS-ISAO to implement capabilities faster and focus on its core mission of actionable sharing among members. In the future, the LS-ISAO may also be able to take advantage of new solutions and technologies developed by the FS-ISAC and the Depository Trust & Clearing Corporation (DTCC), including a threat-intelligence-sharing platform called Soltra Edge.[6]

At the time of the release of this book, an LS-ISAO member must be a law firm duly licensed or registered with any regulatory body to which it is subject, with at least a majority of its lawyers working and authorized to practice law in the United States, the United Kingdom, or Canada. (These requirements are subject to change by a majority of the members.) To apply, a firm submits an application and is vetted against these criteria. If a firm is approved and accepts the subscriber agreement, then it pays a subscription fee and becomes an LS-ISAO member. Currently, the benefits include the following:

- participation on an intelligence-sharing list server providing relevant and actionable threat alerts, vulnerabilities, and advisories from vendors and government agencies;
- access to a list of participating law firms;
- receipt of a monthly LS-ISAO report;
- a monthly member meeting;

[5] GAO, *Bank and Other Depository Regulators Need Better Data Analytics and Depository Institutions Want More Usable Threat Information* (July 2, 2015), http://www.gao.gov/products/GAO-15-509.

[6] Soltra, *Soltra Launches New Membership Program for Soltra Edge Users*, Press Release (Sept. 9, 2015), https://www.fsisac.com/sites/default/files/news/Soltra%20Press%20Release%20Membership%20Model%20FINAL%203.pdf.

- a way for members to submit information directly to an independent party;
- crisis notification and coordination;
- participation in member surveys; and
- participation in LS-ISAO events.

Sharing information is encouraged but not mandatory. To ensure that shared information is protected, each member agrees to comply with the LS-ISAO's "Traffic Light Protocol," a method used in information sharing to keep certain information private. Using the colors of a traffic light, the originator of the information assigns to it a "classification" that determines if and how it can be shared with others.

LS-ISAO members are currently receiving relevant and actionable threat information alerts, vulnerabilities, and advisories. Recently, an intelligence report identified several law firms as the targets of cybercriminal activity, and the LS-ISAO was able to respond quickly and disseminate the intelligence to each firm individually. In the event of a crisis, a crisis notification system is also in place to bring the members together to address their needs. As the LS-ISAO grows, it will likely engage in threat automation and threat exercises; and in general, its level of sophistication will increase to combat increasingly sophisticated threats.

Law firms can share all types of information that may be beneficial to the community. If desired, they can share indicators about cyber threats such as malicious sites, known malware, denial-of-service attacks, phishing, or a combination of these; and they can share information about software vulnerabilities that pertain to the legal industry. Information sharing and analysis sharing help law firms understand the changing threat environment, develop stronger controls, and respond more effectively to threats and attacks. Information about physical threats ranging from hurricanes to geopolitical intelligence can be shared as well. Because cyberattacks have the potential to cause serious physical damage, and because physical intrusions can severely compromise cybersecurity, physical security is in fact becoming increasingly integrated with cybersecurity.[7] Whether the two are isolated or integrated, an understanding of both cyber and physical threats helps law firms protect their own as well as their clients' businesses and improves their response to incidents.

Depending on the type of information, LS-ISAO members can share information solely between two specific members, between larger "circles of trust" (groups comprised of multiple firms), or with the entire community (if appropriate). Following the Traffic Light Protocol, the member providing the information determines how that information is distributed. A member can submit a report to an LS-ISAO security analyst either with attribution or anonymously, or directly to another member. Generally speaking, as an ISAO matures, such circles of trust foster collaboration among certain common interest groups, such as organizations with similar functional needs (e.g., business resiliency) or working in certain industries (e.g., compliance and auditing).

Typically, ISAOs also put mechanisms in place for proper information sharing between the private sector and government entities, including law enforcement and the

[7] *E.g.*, Stuxnet.

intelligence community. As one of the sources of information for intelligence, the government also shares information that can be useful for combating threats. The LS-ISAO is able to leverage the FS-ISAC's established processes for receiving and analyzing information from the government.[8]

Information shared within the LS-ISAO goes into a centralized, highly secure repository of threat indicators. Over time, this becomes a knowledge base that can help firms understand what types of threats and attacks are trending and evolving, and how the firms' cyber defenses should evolve to meet them. Collective intelligence is gathered from various open-source sites. When appropriate, information is put into an alert and distributed to the membership. Submissions are made directly to an LS-ISAO analyst, either over the telephone or via email; or members can submit anonymous submissions directly through an LS-ISAO portal. The analyst gathers the submitted information, scrubs it of details that would allow attribution to the source, and returns it to the originator for final approval before disseminating it to the membership.

The LS-ISAO has grown substantially in a short time. It is already sharing timely cyber and physical security information and analysis among law firms to help protect the community from cyber and physical threats. This has resulted in greater resilience, integrity, and stability for LS-ISAO members, and has improved their ability to provide critical services to the community. Since 2017, the LS-ISAO has been a member community of the cross-sector Global Resilience Federation. See https://grfederation.org/ls-isao.

[8] As noted earlier, the DHS is actively assisting ISAOs and ISACs through a strengthened cyber information and sharing program. See https://www.dhs.gov/ciscp.

CHAPTER 8

HOW COURTS CAN USE THE CYBERSECURITY FRAMEWORK FOR CRITICAL INFRASTRUCTURE

Daniel Garrie, Esq. and Judge Leo M. Gordon

§ 8.01 Introduction

§ 8.02 Overview of the NIST Framework

§ 8.03 The Framework Core: Functions of a Successful Cybersecurity Program
- [A] Identify
- [B] Protect
- [C] Detect
- [D] Respond
- [E] Recover

§ 8.04 Assessing Cybersecurity Risk Management Practices Using the Framework Implementation Tiers
- [A] The Framework Implementation Tiers
- [B] The Framework Profiles: Snapshots of an Organization's Cybersecurity Practices

§ 8.01 INTRODUCTION

Because they store large amounts of personal or business-proprietary information, courts are under increasing pressure to ensure the safety of that information. Breaches can—and have—occurred through compromises at law firms and third-party vendors. Because courts have access to the most important information about law firms and their clients, courts are increasingly seen as threat vectors. In the financial services sector alone, the Office of the Comptroller of the Currency, the Securities and Exchange Commission, the Consumer Financial Protection Bureau, the Commodity Futures Trading Commission, and the New York Department of Financial Services (among others) have emphasized the importance of managing third-party risk. It is important for courts to have the security policies and procedures in place to protect litigant information appropriately.

There are many standards relating to policies and procedures for information security (IS) programs. The private sector has historically relied on the International Organization for Standardization (ISO) standards 27001 and 27002 as the basis for information security practices. However, government contractors who provide products or services to federal agencies are required to comply with the Federal Information Security Management Act (FISMA) first enacted in 2002 and updated in December, 2014.[1] FISMA assigns responsibility for developing detailed security standards for federal computer systems to the National Institute of Standards and Technology (NIST).[2] Since 2002, NIST has been developing cybersecurity standards and constantly revising them to address ever-changing cyber threats. Most federal agencies as well as their contractors are required to follow a standard set forth in NIST Special Publication 800-53 Revision 4 (NIST 800-53).

In February, 2013, President Obama issued Executive Order (EO) 13636, "Improving Critical Infrastructure Cybersecurity," which directed NIST to work with stakeholders to develop a voluntary framework for reducing cyber risks to critical infrastructure. On February 12, 2014, NIST issued version 1 of the Framework for Improving Critical Infrastructure Cybersecurity (the Framework). The EO is applicable to infrastructure (including utilities that provide energy and water) as well as sectors that span transportation, financial services, communications, health care and public health, food and agriculture, chemical and other facilities, dams, key manufacturers, emergency services, and several others. Third-party vendors covered by the EO are subject to a request to provide information to their sector's federal overseers as to policies and procedures they have in place to meet the Framework's requirements.

NIST cybersecurity standards are recognized forerunners in information security benchmarking and have been widely adopted by a variety of entities looking for cybersecurity guidance both inside and outside the Federal Government.[3] As a result, States

---

[1] 40 U.S.C. § 11331; 44 U.S.C. § 3544; 15 U.S.C. §§ 278g-3, 278g-4. This statutory standard applies to many government contractors, thus extending its sphere over a portion of the private sector. 44 U.S.C. § 3544(a) and (b).

[2] 44 U.S.C. § 3544; 40 U.S.C. § 11331(b)(1)(C).

[3] *See* Debevoise & Plimpton, New *Federal Guidance on Cybersecurity for Mobile Devices* (Feb. 9, 2015), http://www.debevoise.com/~/media/files/insights/publications/2015/11/20151109_new_federal_guidance_on_cybersecurity.pdf; *See also,* National Association of Insurance Commissioners, *Principles for Effective Cybersecurity: Insurance Regulatory Guidance*, http://www.naic.org/documents/committees_ex_cyber security_tf_final_principles_for_cybersecurity_guidance.pdf.

have begun to leverage the Framework to improve the security of their infrastructures,[4] overseers have been utilizing it to assess the strength of information security policies and procedures,[5] technology companies have been developing products and services to align with it,[6] and major insurance providers have begun to offer policies tied to the Framework.[7]

It seems inevitable that courts will start requesting information from law firms (and others involved in the litigation process) about how their information security programs compare to the Framework. These entities will in turn request similar information from those in their supply chains, and so on. In short, the Framework may rapidly become the de facto document for comparison and assessment of cybersecurity programs in the United States. Courts and law firms may find the NIST standard instructive as they develop information security programs.

This chapter provides an overview of the NIST Framework before discussing some of the ways courts and law firms may use it and other NIST standards. The chapter concludes by examining some of the effects the NIST Framework has had since it was issued.

§ 8.02 OVERVIEW OF THE NIST FRAMEWORK

The NIST Framework consists of three primary components: (1) the Framework Core, which sets out the basic functions of a successful cybersecurity program; (2) the Framework Implementation Tiers, which provide guidance in assessing an organization's cybersecurity practices; and (3) the Framework Profiles, which help organizations develop an overview of how their cybersecurity goals fit into the overall goals, needs, and operations of the organization.[8]

§ 8.03 THE FRAMEWORK CORE: FUNCTIONS OF A SUCCESSFUL CYBERSECURITY PROGRAM

The Framework Core describes cybersecurity functions that all kinds of organizations employ to achieve specific security outcomes. It also gives examples of existing standards

[4] *See* https://www.nist.gov/cyberframework/state-local-tribal-and-territorial-perspectives.

[5] FFIEC, *FFIEC Cybersecurity Assessment Tool* (June 20, 2015), https://www.ffiec.gov/pdf/cybersecurity/FFIEC_CAT_CEO_Board_Overview_June_2015_PDF1.pdf; U.S. Securities and Exchange Commission, Division of Investment Management, *IM Guidance Update: Cybersecurity Guidance (No. 2015-02)* (Apr. 2015), https://www.sec.gov/investment/im-guidance-2015-02.pdf; U.S. Department of Energy, Office of Electricity Delivery & Energy Reliability, *Reducing Cyber Risk to Critical Infrastructure: NIST Framework*, http://energy.gov/oe/services/cybersecurity/reducing-cyber-risk-critical-infrastructure-nist-framework; U.S. Department of Health and Human Services, Office for Civil Rights, *Addressing Gaps in Cybersecurity: OCR Releases Crosswalk Between HIPAA Security Rule and NIST Cybersecurity Framework*, http://www.hhs.gov/hipaa/for-professionals/security/nist-security-hipaa-crosswalk/.

[6] IBM, *IBM to Help Companies Utilize New Cybersecurity Framework Aimed at Protecting Nation's Critical Infrastructure*, https://newsroom.ibm.com/2014-02-14-IBM-to-Help-Companies-Utilize-New-Cybersecurity-Framework-Aimed-at-Protecting-Nations-Critical-Infrastructure.

[7] American Bankers Association, *2016 Cyber Insurance Buying Guide*, http://www.aba.com/Tools/Function/Documents/2016Cyber-Insurance-Buying-Guide_FINAL.pdf.

[8] National Institute of Standards and Technology, *Framework for Improving Critical Infrastructure Cybersecurity* (Feb. 12, 2014).

to facilitate the implementation of those functions. At a high level, it essentially answers a significant question: What do we want our cybersecurity risk management program to do? Courts and law firms that do not have a comprehensive cybersecurity program in place may use the Framework Core to determine what their cybersecurity risk management program should achieve. Of course, any program should be adjusted in accordance with the size of the court (or law firm) and scope of its work.

The Framework Core addresses five basic functions to be included in an organization's cybersecurity risk management program:

- *Identification.* Understand the systems in use and engage in risk assessment and asset management.
- *Protection.* Develop safeguards for delivery of critical infrastructure services (e.g., training, data security, and access control).
- *Detection.* Perform detection and monitoring activities to identify cybersecurity events.
- *Response.* Create action plans for responding to and mitigating cybersecurity events.
- *Recovery.* Restore damaged capabilities and make improvements after an incident.

These five functions should serve as part of a guiding principle for courts; they are not intended to form a serial path or lead to a desired, static end-state. When addressing these functions, it is important for courts to realize that, ideally, they should answer the question of the program's goals concurrently and continuously in order to form an operational culture that addresses the dynamic cybersecurity risk.

These five functions are divided into categories and subcategories for maximum specificity. The subdivisions further delineate each of the five functions based on cybersecurity outcomes that are tied to programmatic needs and particular activities. Examples of categories include "asset management," "access control," and "detection processes." Subcategories further divide a category into specific outcomes of technical, management, or shared technical and management activities. They provide a set of results that, although not exhaustive, help support achievement of the outcomes in each category. Examples of subcategories include: "External information systems are catalogued," "Data-at-rest is protected," and "Notifications from detection systems are investigated."

The Framework is set up to accommodate multiple standards that organizations use, including the ISO 27001 and NIST 800-53 standards as well as a number of others. Each of the specific section references within such standards is delineated such that an organization can compare it to the other standards. However, inclusion of the various sections within topical areas under each of the five functions makes it easier for an organization to build or to assess the comprehensiveness of its cybersecurity program.

These five functions contained in the Framework should be tailored to a court. The tailoring should account for the court's size, location, and operations. The Framework is flexible and invites courts to adapt it substantially to suit the specific needs of each. Table 8-1 sets forth the entire Framework Core.[9]

[9] National Institute of Standards and Technology, *Framework for Improving Critical Infrastructure Cybersecurity* (Feb. 12, 2014).

TABLE 8-1:
Framework Core: Asset Management

<table>
<tr><td rowspan="29">IDENTIFY (ID)</td><td rowspan="29">Asset Management (ID.AM): The data, personnel, devices, systems, and facilities that enable the organization to achieve business purposes are identified and managed consistent with their relative importance to business objectives and the organization's risk strategy.</td><td rowspan="6">ID.AM-1: Physical devices and systems within the organization are inventoried</td><td>CCS CSC 1</td></tr>
<tr><td>COBIT 5 BAI09.01, BAI09.02</td></tr>
<tr><td>ISA 62443-2-1:2009 4.2.3.4</td></tr>
<tr><td>ISA 62443-3-3:2013 SR 7.8</td></tr>
<tr><td>ISO/IEC 27001:2013 A.8.1.1, A.8.1.2</td></tr>
<tr><td>NIST SP 800-53 Rev. 4 CM-8</td></tr>
<tr><td rowspan="6">ID.AM-2: Software platforms and applications within the organization are inventoried</td><td>CCS CSC 2</td></tr>
<tr><td>COBIT 5 BAI09.01, BAI09.02, BAI09.05</td></tr>
<tr><td>ISA 62443-2-1:2009 4.2.3.4</td></tr>
<tr><td>ISA 62443-3-3:2013 SR 7.8</td></tr>
<tr><td>ISO/IEC 27001:2013 A.8.1.1, A.8.1.2</td></tr>
<tr><td>NIST SP 800-53 Rev. 4 CM-8</td></tr>
<tr><td rowspan="5">ID.AM-3: Organizational communication and data flows are mapped</td><td>CCS CSC 1</td></tr>
<tr><td>COBIT 5 DSS05.02</td></tr>
<tr><td>ISA 62443-2-1:2009 4.2.3.4</td></tr>
<tr><td>ISO/IEC 27001:2013 A.13.2.1</td></tr>
<tr><td>NIST SP 800-53 Rev. 4 AC-4, CA-3, CA-9, PL-8</td></tr>
<tr><td rowspan="3">ID.AM-4: External information systems are catalogued</td><td>COBIT 5 APO02.02</td></tr>
<tr><td>ISO/IEC 27001:2013 A.11.2.6</td></tr>
<tr><td>NIST SP 800-53 Rev. 4 AC-20, SA-9</td></tr>
<tr><td rowspan="4">ID.AM-5: Resources (e.g., hardware, devices, data, and software) are prioritized based on their classification, criticality, and business value</td><td>COBIT 5 APO03.03, APO03.04, BAI09.02</td></tr>
<tr><td>ISA 62443-2-1:2009 4.2.3.6</td></tr>
<tr><td>ISO/IEC 27001:2013 A.8.2.1</td></tr>
<tr><td>NIST SP 800-53 Rev. 4 CP-2, RA-2, SA-14</td></tr>
<tr><td rowspan="5">ID.AM-6: Cybersecurity roles and responsibilities for the entire workforce and third-party stakeholders (e.g., suppliers, customers, partners) are established</td><td>COBIT 5 APO01.02, DSS06.03</td></tr>
<tr><td>ISA 62443-2-1:2009 4.3.2.3.3</td></tr>
<tr><td>ISO/IEC 27001:2013 A.6.1.1</td></tr>
<tr><td>NIST SP 800-53 Rev. 4 CP-2, PS-7, PM-11</td></tr>
</table>

[A] Identify

The Framework Core section on identification begins with asset management (ID.AM), which directs organizations to identify data assets, understand the flow of data, and prioritize their data assets based on a variety of factors. Courts and any other organization that is serious about securing its data must undertake this step in order to understand their data assets as well as how data flows. Another critical element of this provision is the classification of data assets, which is a prominent consideration throughout the entire Framework Core.

The section then goes on to direct organizations to identify the business environment (ID.BE) they are operating in—specifically, the organization's place in the national critical infrastructure (see table 8-2). Furthermore, this step affords an organization the opportunity to understand the mechanics of its work and possible implications for its cybersecurity policies. It is essential for a court to recognize that while critically important, the Framework Core is ultimately not the center of its work. The importance to the court of identifying its role is so that it properly understands how the NIST Framework Core can help ensure a smooth path to fulfilling that role. Courts must understand this principle both in designing their own cybersecurity systems as well as in encouraging law firms and others involved in the litigation process to do the same.

TABLE 8-2:
Framework Core: Business Environment

<table>
<tr><td rowspan="8">IDENTIFY (ID)</td><td rowspan="8">Business Environment (ID.BE): The organization's mission, objectives, stakeholders, and activities are understood and prioritized; this information is used to inform cybersecurity roles, responsibilities, and risk management decisions.</td><td rowspan="3">ID.BE-1: The organization's role in the supply chain is identified and communicated</td><td>COBIT 5 APO08.04, APO08.05, APO10.03, APO10.04, APO10.05</td></tr>
<tr><td>ISO/IEC 27001:2013 A.15.1.3, A.15.2.1, A.15.2.2</td></tr>
<tr><td>NIST SP 800-53 Rev. 4 CP-2, SA-12</td></tr>
<tr><td rowspan="2">ID.BE-2: The organization's place in critical infrastructure and its industry sector are identified and communicated</td><td>COBIT 5 APO02.06, APO03.01</td></tr>
<tr><td>NIST SP 800-53 Rev. 4 PM-8</td></tr>
<tr><td rowspan="3">ID.BE-3: Priorities for organizational mission, objectives, and activities are established and communicated</td><td>COBIT 5 APO02.01, APO02.06, APO03.01</td></tr>
<tr><td>ISA 62443-2-1:2009 4.2.2.1, 4.2.3.6</td></tr>
<tr><td>NIST SP 800-53 Rev. 4 PM-11, SA-14</td></tr>
</table>

TABLE 8-2: (cont'd)

	ID.BE-4: Dependencies and critical functions for delivery of critical services are established	**ISO/IEC 27001:2013** A.11.2.2, A.11.2.3, A.12.1.3
		NIST SP 800-53 Rev. 4 CP-8, PE-9, PE-11, PM-8, SA-14
	ID.BE-5: Resilience requirements to support delivery of critical services are established	**COBIT 5** DSS04.02
		ISO/IEC 27001:2013 A.11.1.4, A.17.1.1, A.17.1.2, A.17.2.1
		NIST SP 800-53 Rev. 4 CP-2, CP-11, SA-14

Next, the Framework Core turns to governance (ID.GV; see table 8-3). Here, it directs organizations to identify and establish procedures to manage and monitor the various requirements that may inform their cybersecurity policies. This section also directs organizations to identify all of the legal duties and policy directives they may be subject to and how these requirements are being managed. This step is uniquely important for courts because it forces them to identify applicable laws and policies. Furthermore, a court during this step will begin to identify how its cybersecurity processes actually address the risks it faces, and this in turn will reveal any gaps to be addressed subsequently (per the Framework Core).

TABLE 8-3:
Framework Core: Governance

IDENTIFY (ID)	**Governance (ID.GV):** The policies, procedures, and processes to manage and monitor the organization's regulatory, legal, risk, environmental, and operational requirements are understood and inform the management of cybersecurity risk.	**ID.GV-1:** Organizational information security policy is established	**COBIT 5** APO01.03, EDM01.01, EDM01.02
			ISA 62443-2-1:2009 4.3.2.6
			ISO/IEC 27001:2013 A.5.1.1
			NIST SP 800-53 Rev. 4-1 controls from all families
		ID.GV-2: Information security roles and responsibilities are coordinated and aligned with internal roles and external partners	**COBIT 5** APO13.12
			ISA 62443-2-1:2009 4.3.2.3.3
			ISO/IEC 27001:2013 A.6.1.1, A.7.2.1
			NIST SP 800-53 Rev. 4 PM-1, PS-7
		ID.GV-3: Legal and regulatory requirements regarding cybersecurity, including privacy and civil liberties obligations, are understood and managed	**COBIT 5** MEA03.01, MEA03.04
			ISA 62443-2-1:2009 4.4.3.7
			ISO/IEC 27001:2013 A.18.1
			NIST SP 800-53 Rev. 4-1 controls from all families (except PM-1)

TABLE 8-3: (cont'd)

	ID.GV-4: Governance and risk management processes address cybersecurity risks	**COBIT 5** DSS04.02
		ISA 62443-2-1:2009 4.2.3.1, 4.2.3.3, 4.2.3.8, 4.2.3.9, 4.2.3.11, 4.3.2.4.3, 4.3.2.6.3
		NIST SP 800-53 Rev. 4 PM-9, PM-11

Finally, the Framework Core turns from identifying assets and understanding one's organization to performing a risk assessment (ID.RA; see table 8-4). This critical step directs organizations to determine the threats they may face as well as the likelihood of each and impact should it materialize. This is an important step because it begins to direct an organization's focus toward the threats themselves. Of specific importance is that here—in one overarching step—organizations are both determining the threats they face as well as contextualizing those threats in terms of likelihood and impact. As discussed throughout this book, although courts make a compelling target for cybercriminals, courts cannot be expected to create perfect cybersecurity policies immediately; rather, they must prioritize the greatest risks, eliminate these, and then go down the line addressing the rest. This process is the heart of a court's risk assessment.

TABLE 8-4:
Framework Core: Risk Assessment

IDENTIFY (ID)	**Risk Assessment (ID.RA):** The organization understands the cybersecurity risk to organizational operations (including mission, functions, image, or reputation), organizational assets, and individuals.	**ID.RA-1:** Asset vulnerabilities are identified and documented	**CCS CSC** 4
			COBIT 5 APO12.01, APO12.02, APO12.03, APO12.04
			ISA 62443-2-1:2009 4.2.3, 4.2.3.7, 4.2.3.9, 4.2.3.12
			ISO/IEC 27001:2013 A.12.6.1, A.18.2.3
			NIST SP 800-53 Rev. 4 CA-2, CA-7, CA-8, RA-3, RA-5, SA-5, SA-11, SI-2, SI-4, SI-5
		ID.RA-2: Threat and vulnerability information is received from information-sharing forums and sources	**ISA 62443-2-1:2009** 4.2.3, 4.2.3.9, 4.2.3.12
			ISO/IEC 27001:2013 A.6.1.4
			NIST SP 800-53 Rev. 4 PM-15, PM-16, SI-5

TABLE 8-4: (cont'd)

	ID.RA-3: Threats, both internal and external, are identified and documented	**COBIT 5** APO12.01, APO12.02, APO12.03, APO12.04
		ISA 62443-2-1:2009 4.2.3, 4.2.3.9, 4.2.3.12
		NIST SP 800-53 Rev. 4 RA-3, SI-5, PM-12, PM-16
	ID.RA-4: Potential business impacts and likelihoods are identified	**COBIT 5** DSS04.02
		ISA 62443-2-1:2009 4.2.3, 4.2.3.9, 4.2.3.12
		NIST SP 800-53 Rev. 4 RA-2, RA-3, PM-9, PM-11, SA-14
	ID.RA-5: Threats, vulnerabilities, likelihoods, and impacts are used to determine risk	**COBIT 5** APO12.02
		ISO/IEC 27001:2013 A.12.6.1
		NIST SP 800-53 Rev. 4 RA-2, RA-3, PM-16
	ID.RA-6: Risk responses are identified and prioritized	**COBIT 5** APO12.05, APO13.02
		NIST SP 800-53 Rev. 4 PM-4, PM-9

The identification phase of the Framework Core concludes with a directive that organizations must identify and create a risk management strategy (ID.RM; see table 8-5). This step builds on risk assessment, but now goes a step further to ask the organization to determine and express its risk tolerance. By asking them to determine their risk tolerances, the Framework Core once again demonstrates its applicability to all types of courts. It allows a court to use all of the information it has collected during the prior steps to determine its risk tolerance and to contextualize that tolerance within the judicial sector.

TABLE 8-5:
Framework Core: Risk Management Strategy

IDENTIFY (ID)	**Risk Management Strategy (ID.RM):** The organization's priorities, constraints, risk tolerances, and assumptions are established and used to support operational risk decisions.	**ID.RM-1:** Risk management processes are established, managed, and agreed to by organizational stakeholders	**COBIT 5** APO12.04, APO12.05, APO13.02, BAI02.03, BAI04.02
			ISA 62443-2-1:2009 4.3.4.2
			NIST SP 800-53 Rev. 4 PM-9
		ID.RM-2: Organizational risk tolerance is determined and clearly expressed	**COBIT 5** APO12.06
			ISA 62443-2-1:2009 4.3.2.6.5
			NIST SP 800-53 Rev. 4 PM-9

TABLE 8-5: (cont'd)

	ID.RM-3: The organization's determination of risk tolerance is informed by its role in critical infrastructure and sector-specific risk analysis	**NIST SP 800-53 Rev. 4** PM-8, PM-9, PM-11, SA-14

[B] Protect

The Framework Core next moves from identifying threats and risks to an organization's assets to developing policies and procedures to protect its assets. This process begins with access control (PR.AC; see table 8-6), which directs an organization to limit access to assets and facilities—both local and remote—to authorized individuals only. Courts must pay careful attention to this step because of the uniquely sensitive information they deal with during litigation. While lawyers are officers of the court, and while court staff play vital roles, judges and court management must be able to set permissions to restrict access certain files. Furthermore, there may be many nonlawyers on the network whose access to files should be limited. Additionally, litigation practice is evolving such that remote access is becoming more and more important to everyone participating. This means that remote access must be more carefully managed.

TABLE 8-6:
Framework Core: Protect

PROTECT (PR)	**Access Control (PR.AC):** Access to assets and associated facilities is limited to authorized users, processes, or devices, and to authorized activities and transactions.	**PR.AC-1:** Identities and credentials are managed for authorized devices and users	**CCS CSC** 16
			COBIT 5 DSS05.04, DSS06.03
			ISA 62443-2-1:2009 4.3.3.5.1
			ISA 62443-3-3:2013 SR 1.1, SR 1.2, SR 1.3, SR 1.4, SR 1.5, SR 1.7, SR 1.8, SR 1.9
			ISO/IEC 27001:2013 A.9.2.1, A.9.2.2, A.9.2.4, A.9.3.1, A.9.4.2, A.9.4.3
			NIST SP 800-53 Rev. 4 AC-2, IA Family

TABLE 8-6: (cont'd)

	PR.AC-2: Physical access to assets is managed and protected	**COBIT 5** DSS01.04, DSS05.05
		ISA 62443-2-1:2009 4.3.3.3.2, 4.3.3.3.8
		ISO/IEC 27001:2013 A.11.1.1, A.11.1.2, A.11.1.4, A.11.1.6, A.11.2.3
		NIST SP 800-53 Rev. 4 PE-2, PE-3, PE-4, PE-5, PE-6, PE-9
	PR.AC-3: Remote access is managed	**COBIT 5** APO13.01, DSS01.04, DSS05.03
		ISA 62443-2-1:2009 4.3.3.6.6
		ISA 62443-3-3:2013 SR 1.13, SR 2.6
		ISO/IEC 27001:2013 A.6.2.2, A.13.1.1, A.13.2.1
		NIST SP 800-53 Rev. 4 AC-17, AC-19, AC-20
	PR.AC-4: Access permissions are managed, incorporating the principles of least privilege and separation of duties	**CCS CSC** 12, 15
		ISA 62443-2-1:2009 4.3.3.7.3
		ISA 62443-3-3:2013 SR 2.1
		ISO/IEC 27001:2013 A.6.1.2, A.9.1.2, A.9.2.3, A.9.4.1, A.9.4.4
		NIST SP 800-53 Rev. 4 AC-2, AC-3, AC-5, AC-6, AC-16
	PR.AC-5: Network integrity is protected, incorporating network segregation where appropriate	**ISA 62443-2-1:2009** 4.3.3.4
		ISA 62443-3-3:2013 SR 3.1, SR 3.8
		ISO/IEC 27001:2013 A.13.1.1, A.13.1.3, A.13.2.1
		NIST SP 800-53 Rev. 4 AC-4, SC-7

The next step in protecting assets deals with awareness and training (PR.AT; see table 8-7). Arguably, this is the most important step toward protecting assets within the Framework Core, because—as emphasized throughout this book—untrained individuals pose a huge threat to organizations. Because courts may be particularly vulnerable, they must take heightened precautions to train court staff. Hackers are currently targeting courts to obtain access to data and systems. The first step in the process of stopping them is to train all court staff and ensure that all members of each group of court personnel understand their roles and responsibilities with respect to securing the court and the judiciary as a whole.

TABLE 8-7:
Framework Core: Awareness and Training

Function	Category	Subcategory	Informative References
PROTECT (PR)	**Awareness and Training (PR.AT):** The organization's personnel and partners are provided cybersecurity awareness education and are adequately trained to perform their information security-related duties and responsibilities consistent with related policies, procedures, and agreements.	**PR.AT-1:** All users are informed and trained	**CCS CSC** 9
			COBIT 5 APO07.03, BAI05.07
			ISA 62443-2-1:2009 4.3.2.4.2
			ISO/IEC 27001:2013 A.7.2.2
			NIST SP 800-53 Rev. 4 AT-2, PM-13
		PR.AT-2: Privileged users understand roles and responsibilities	**CCS CSC** 9
			COBIT 5 APO07.02, DSS06.03
			ISA 62443-2-1:2009 4.3.2.4.2, 4.3.2.4.3
			ISO/IEC 27001:2013 A.6.1.1, A.7.2.2
			NIST SP 800-53 Rev. 4 AT-3, PM-13
		PR.AT-3: Third-party stakeholders, if any (e.g., suppliers, customers, partners) understand roles and responsibilities	**CCS CSC** 9
			COBIT 5 APO07.03, APO10.04, APO10.05
			ISA 62443-2-1:2009 4.3.2.4.2
			ISO/IEC 27001:2013 A.6.1.1, A.7.2.2
			NIST SP 800-53 Rev. 4 PS-7, SA-9
		PR.AT-4: Senior management understands roles and responsibilities	**CCS CSC** 9
			COBIT 5 APO07.03
			ISA 62443-2-1:2009 4.3.2.4.2
			ISO/IEC 27001:2013 A.6.1.1, A.7.2.2
			NIST SP 800-53 Rev. 4 AT-3, PM-13
		PR.AT-5: Physical and information security personnel understand roles and responsibilities	**CCS CSC** 9
			COBIT 5 APO07.03
			ISA 62443-2-1:2009 4.3.2.4.2
			ISO/IEC 27001:2013 A.6.1.1, A.7.2.2
			NIST SP 800-53 Rev. 4 AT-3, PM-13

Next, the Framework Core turns to data security (PR.DS; see table 8-8), wherein organizations are directed to manage their data in a way that is consistent with the risk strategies they have determined during the identification process described earlier. In the interest of ensuring the integrity of an organization's software, firmware, and assets, this section breaks down each type of data asset that must be protected. Data security must be a priority for all courts.

TABLE 8-8:
Framework Core: Data Security

<table>
<tr><td rowspan="20">PROTECT (PR)</td><td rowspan="20">Data Security (PR.DS): Information and records (data) are managed consistent with the organization's risk strategy to protect the confidentiality, integrity, and availability of information.</td><td rowspan="5">PR.DS-1: Data-at-rest is protected</td><td>CCS CSC 17</td></tr>
<tr><td>COBIT 5 APO01.06, BAI02.01, BAI06.01, DSS06.06</td></tr>
<tr><td>ISA 62443-3-3:2013 SR 3.4, SR 4.1</td></tr>
<tr><td>ISO/IEC 27001:2013 A.8.2.3</td></tr>
<tr><td>NIST SP 800-53 Rev. 4 SC-28</td></tr>
<tr><td rowspan="5">PR.DS-2: Data-in-transit is protected</td><td>CCS CSC 17</td></tr>
<tr><td>COBIT 5 APO01.06, DSS06.06</td></tr>
<tr><td>ISA 62443-3-3:2013 SR 3.1, SR 3.8, SR 4.1, SR 4.2</td></tr>
<tr><td>ISO/IEC 27001:2013 A.8.2.3, A.13.1.1, A.13.2.1, A.13.2.3, A.14.1.2, A.14.1.3</td></tr>
<tr><td>NIST SP 800-53 Rev. 4 SC-8</td></tr>
<tr><td rowspan="5">PR.DS-3: Assets are formally managed throughout removal, transfers, and disposition</td><td>COBIT 5 BAI09.03</td></tr>
<tr><td>ISA 62443-2-1:2009 4. 4.3.3.3.9, 4.3.4.4.1</td></tr>
<tr><td>ISA 62443-3-3:2013 SR 4.2</td></tr>
<tr><td>ISO/IEC 27001:2013 A.8.2.3, A.8.3.1, A.8.3.2, A.8.3.3, A.11.2.7</td></tr>
<tr><td>NIST SP 800-53 Rev. 4 CM-8, MP-6, PE-16</td></tr>
<tr><td rowspan="4">PR.DS-4: Adequate capacity to ensure availability is maintained</td><td>COBIT 5 APO13.01</td></tr>
<tr><td>ISA 62443-3-3:2013 SR 7.1, SR 7.2</td></tr>
<tr><td>ISO/IEC 27001:2013 A.12.3.1</td></tr>
<tr><td>NIST SP 800-53 Rev. 4 AU-4, CP-2, SC-5</td></tr>
</table>

TABLE 8-8: (cont'd)

	PR.DS-5: Protections against data leaks are implemented	**CCS CSC** 17
		COBIT 5 APO01.06
		ISA 62443-3-3:2013 SR 5.2
		ISO/IEC 27001:2013 A.6.1.2, A.7.1.1, A.7.1.2, A.7.3.1, A.8.2.2, A.8.2.3, A.9.1.1, A.9.1.2, A.9.2.3, A.9.4.1, A.9.4.4, A.9.4.5, A.13.1.3, A.13.2.1, A.13.2.3, A.13.2.4, A.14.1.2, A.14.1.3
		NIST SP 800-53 Rev. 4 AC-4, AC-5, AC-6, PE-19, PS-3, PS-6, SC-7, SC-8, SC-13, SC-31, SI-4
	PR.DS-6: Integrity checking mechanisms are used to verify software, firmware, and information integrity	**ISA 62443-3-3:2013** SR 3.1, SR 3.3, SR 3.4, SR 3.8
		ISO/IEC 27001:2013 A.12.2.1, A.12.5.1, A.14.1.2, A.14.1.3
		NIST SP 800-53 Rev. 4 SI-7
	PR.DS-7: The development and testing environment(s) are separate from the production environment	**COBIT 5** BAI07.04
		ISO/IEC 27001:2013 A.12.1.4
		NIST SP 800-53 Rev. 4 CM-2

We next turn to developing information protection processes and procedures (PR.IP; see table 8-9), a step wherein organizations are directed to develop processes to protect data throughout the entire data lifecycle. Courts must remember that data continues to exist even when it is not sitting on the staff's desktops. Data must be managed throughout its lifecycle; even the destruction of data must be carefully secured. As long as the data exists, hackers can attempt to gain access to it. Courts must therefore create policies and procedures ensuring the security of that data. Importantly, courts must also update these policies regularly in order to stay current with threats they may face as well as to prepare for the potential fallout from a data breach.

TABLE 8-9:
Framework Core: Information Protection Processes and Procedures

PROTECT (PR)	**Information Protection Processes and Procedures (PR.IP):** Security policies (that address purpose, scope, roles, responsibilities, management commitment, and coordination among organizational entities), processes, and procedures are maintained and used to manage protection of information systems and assets.	**PR.IP-1:** A baseline configuration of information technology and industrial control systems is created and maintained	**CCS CSC** 3, 10
			COBIT 5 BAI10.01, BAI10.02, BAI10.03, BAI10.05
			ISA 62443-2-1:2009 4.3.4.3.2, 4.3.4.3.3
			ISA 62443-3-3:2013 SR 7.6
			ISO/IEC 27001:2013 A.12.1.2, A.12.5.1, A.12.6.2, A.14.2.2, A.14.2.3, A.14.2.4
			NIST SP 800-53 Rev. 4 CM-2, CM-3, CM-4, CM-5, CM-6, CM-7, CM-9, SA-10
		PR.IP-2: A system development life cycle to manage systems is implemented	**COBIT 5** APO13.01
			ISA 62443-2-1:2009 4.3.4.3.3
			ISO/IEC 27001:2013 A.6.1.5, A.14.1.1, A.14.2.1, A.14.2.5
			NIST SP 800-53 Rev. 4 SA-3, SA-4, SA-8, SA-10, SA-11, SA-12, SA-15, SA-17, PL-8
		PR.IP-3: Configuration change control processes are in place	**COBIT 5** BAI06.01, BAI01.06
			ISA 62443-2-1:2009 4.3.4.3.2, 4.3.4.3.3
			ISA 62443-3-3:2013 SR 7.6
			ISO/IEC 27001:2013 A.12.1.2, A.12.5.1, A.12.6.2, A.14.2.2, A.14.2.3, A.14.2.4
			NIST SP 800-53 Rev. 4 CM-3, CM-4, SA-10
		PR.IP-4: Backups of information are conducted, maintained, and tested periodically	**COBIT 5** APO13.01
			ISA 62443-2-1:2009 4.3.4.3.9
			ISA 62443-3-3:2013 SR 7.3, SR 7.4
			ISO/IEC 27001:2013 A.12.3.1, A.17.1.2A.17.1.3, A.18.1.3
			NIST SP 800-53 Rev. 4 CP-4, CP-6, CP-9

TABLE 8-9: (cont'd)

	PR.IP-5: Policy and regulations regarding the physical operating environment for organizational assets are met	**COBIT 5** DSS01.04, DSS05.05
		ISA 62443-2-1:2009 4.3.3.3.1 4.3.3.3.2, 4.3.3.3.3, 4.3.3.3.5, 4.3.3.3.6
		ISO/IEC 27001:2013 A.11.1.4, A.11.2.1, A.11.2.2, A.11.2.3
		NIST SP 800-53 Rev. 4 PE-10, PE-12, PE-13, PE-14, PE-15, PE-18
	PR.IP-6: Data is destroyed according to policy	**COBIT 5** BAI09.03
		ISA 62443-2-1:2009 4.3.4.4.4
		ISA 62443-3-3:2013 SR 4.2
		ISO/IEC 27001:2013 A.8.2.3, A.8.3.1, A.8.3.2, A.11.2.7
		NIST SP 800-53 Rev. 4 MP-6
	PR.IP-7: Protection processes are continuously improved	**COBIT 5** APO11.06, DSS04.05
		ISA 62443-2-1:2009 4.4.3.1, 4.4.3.2, 4.4.3.3, 4.4.3.4, 4.4.3.5, 4.4.3.6, 4.4.3.7, 4.4.3.8
		NIST SP 800-53 Rev. 4 CA-2, CA-7, CP-2, IR-8, PL-2, PM-6
	PR.IP-8: Effectiveness of protection technologies is shared with appropriate parties	**ISO/IEC 27001:2013** A.16.1.6
		NIST SP 800-53 Rev. 4 AC-21, CA-7, SI-4
	PR.IP-9: Response plans (incident response and business continuity) and recovery plans (incident recovery and disaster recovery) are in place and managed	**COBIT 5** DSS04.03
		ISA 62443-2-1:2009 4.3.2.5.3, 4.3.4.5.1
		ISO/IEC 27001:2013 A.16.1.1, A.17.1.1, A.17.1.2
		NIST SP 800-53 Rev. 4 CP-2, IR-8
	PR.IP-10: Response and recovery plans are tested	**ISA 62443-2-1:2009** 4.3.2.5.7, 4.3.4.5.11
		ISA 62443-3-3:2013 SR 3.3
		ISO/IEC 27001:2013 A.17.1.3
		NIST SP 800-53 Rev.4 CP-4, IR-3, PM-14

TABLE 8-9: (cont'd)

	PR.IP-11: Cybersecurity is included in human resources practices (e.g., deprovisioning, personnel screening)	**COBIT 5** APO07.01, APO07.02, APO07.03, APO07.04, APO07.05
		ISA 62443-2-1:2009 4.3.3.2.1, 4.3.3.2.2, 4.3.3.2.3
		ISO/IEC 27001:2013 A.7.1.1, A.7.3.1, A.8.1.4
		NIST SP 800-53 Rev. 4 PS Family
	PR.IP-12: A vulnerability management plan is developed and implemented	**ISO/IEC 27001:2013** A.12.6.1, A.18.2.2
		NIST SP 800-53 Rev. 4 RA-3, RA-5, SI-2

The penultimate step in protecting data is securing proper maintenance of a court's computer systems (PR.MA; see table 8-10). Computer systems must be maintained regularly to ensure that they are working as intended. Of particular importance to courts is a special focus on remote maintenance in order to ensure there is no unauthorized access.

TABLE 8-10:
Framework Core: Maintenance

PROTECT (PR)	**Maintenance (PR.MA):** Maintenance and repairs of industrial control and information system components are performed consistent with policies and procedures.	**PR.MA-1:** Maintenance and repair of organizational assets is performed and logged in a timely manner, with approved and controlled tools	**COBIT 5** BAI09.03
			ISA 62443-2-1:2009 4.3.3.3.7
			ISO/IEC 27001:2013 A.11.1.2, A.11.2.4, A.11.2.5
			NIST SP 800-53 Rev. 4 MA-2, MA-3, MA-5
		PR.MA-2: Remote maintenance of organizational assets is approved, logged, and performed in a manner that prevents unauthorized access	**COBIT 5** DSS05.04
			ISA 62443-2-1:2009 4.3.3.6.5, 4.3.3.6.6, 4.3.3.6.7, 4.4.4.6.8
			ISO/IEC 27001:2013 A.11.2.4, A.15.1.1, A.15.2.1
			NIST SP 800-53 Rev. 4 MA-4

The "protection" section of the Framework Core concludes with protective technology (PR.PT; see table 8-11). During this step, organizations are directed to ensure the security and resilience of their systems. This step requires regular auditing to ensure that the policies established as a result of the previous steps are being followed.

TABLE 8-11:
Framework Core: Protective Technology

<table>
<tr><td rowspan="14">PROTECT (PR)</td><td rowspan="14">Protective Technology (PR.PT): Technical security solutions are managed to ensure the security and resilience of systems and assets consistent with related policies, procedures, and agreements.</td><td rowspan="6">PR.PT-1: Audit and log records are determined, documented, implemented, and reviewed in accordance with policy</td><td>CCS CSC 14</td></tr>
<tr><td>COBIT 5 APO11.04</td></tr>
<tr><td>ISA 62443-2-1:2009 4.3.3.3.9, 4.3.3.5.8, 4.3.4.4.7, 4.4.2.1, 4.4.2.2, 4.4.2.4</td></tr>
<tr><td>ISA 62443-3-3:2013 SR 2.8, SR 2.9, SR 2.10, SR 2.11, SR 2.12</td></tr>
<tr><td>ISO/IEC 27001:2013 A.12.4.1, A.12.4.2, A.12.4.3, A.12.4.4, A.12.7.1</td></tr>
<tr><td>NIST SP 800-53 Rev. 4 AU Family</td></tr>
<tr><td rowspan="4">PR.PT-2: Removable media is protected and its use restricted according to policy</td><td>COBIT 5 DSS05.02, APO13.01</td></tr>
<tr><td>ISA 62443-3-3:2013 SR 2.3</td></tr>
<tr><td>ISO/IEC 27001:2013 A.8.2.2, A.8.2.3, A.8.3.1, A.8.3.3, A.11.2.9</td></tr>
<tr><td>NIST SP 800-53 Rev. 4 MP-2, MP-4, MP-5, MP-7</td></tr>
<tr><td rowspan="4">PR.PT-3: Access to systems and assets is controlled, incorporating the principle of least functionality</td><td>COBIT 5 DSS05.02</td></tr>
<tr><td>ISA 62443-2-1:2009 4.3.3.5.1, 4.3.3.5.2, 4.3.3.5.3, 4.3.3.5.4, 4.3.3.5.5, 4.3.3.5.6, 4.3.3.5.7, 4.3.3.5.8, 4.3.3.6.1, 4.3.3.6.2, 4.3.3.6.3, 4.3.3.6.4, 4.3.3.6.5, 4.3.3.6.6, 4.3.3.6.7, 4.3.3.6.8, 4.3.3.6.9, 4.3.3.7.1, 4.3.3.7.2, 4.3.3.7.3, 4.3.3.7.4</td></tr>
<tr><td>ISA 62443-3-3:2013 SR 1.1, SR 1.2, SR 1.3, SR 1.4, SR 1.5, SR 1.6, SR 1.7, SR 1.8, SR 1.9, SR 1.10, SR 1.11, SR 1.12, SR 1.13, SR 2.1, SR 2.2, SR 2.3, SR 2.4, SR 2.5, SR 2.6, SR 2.7</td></tr>
<tr><td>ISO/IEC 27001:2013 A.9.1.2</td></tr>
<tr><td></td><td></td><td></td><td>NIST SP 800-53 Rev. 4 AC-3, CM-7</td></tr>
</table>

TABLE 8-11: (cont'd)

	PR.PT-4: Communications and control networks are protected	**CCS CSC** 7
		COBIT 5 DSS05.02, APO13.01
		ISA 62443-3-3:2013 SR 3.1, SR 3.5, SR 3.8, SR 4.1, SR 4.3, SR 5.1, SR 5.2, SR 5.3, SR 7.1, SR 7.6
		ISO/IEC 27001:2013 A.13.1.1, A.13.2.1
		NIST SP 800-53 Rev. 4 AC-4, AC-17, AC-18, CP-8, SC-7

[C] Detect

Once identification and protection are in place, we begin the "detection" section of the Framework Core. Its first concern is to detect anomalies and events (DE.AE; see table 8-12). Whereas the "identification" and "protection" sections are oriented toward creating and developing security policies, this section as well as the following two sections show how a court can detect, respond to, and recover from the inevitable attack—but it must all begin here, with detecting anomalies and events. Having set up adequate detection, courts must then analyze any events and determine their potential impact.

TABLE 8-12:
Framework Core: Anomalies and Events

DETECT (DE)	**Anomalies and Events (DE.AE):** Anomalous activity is detected in a timely manner and the potential impact of events is understood.	**DE.AE-1:** A baseline of network operations and expected data flows for users and systems is established and managed	**COBIT 5** DSS03.01
			ISA 62443-2-1:2009 4.4.3.3
			NIST SP 800-53 Rev. 4 AC-4, CA-3, CM-2, SI-4
		DE.AE-2: Detected events are analyzed to understand attack targets and methods	**ISA 62443-2-1:2009** 4.3.4.5.6, 4.3.4.5.7, 4.3.4.5.8
			ISA 62443-3-3:2013 SR 2.8, SR 2.9, SR 2.10, SR 2.11, SR 2.12, SR 3.9, SR 6.1, SR 6.2
			ISO/IEC 27001:2013 A.16.1.1, A.16.1.4
			NIST SP 800-53 Rev. 4 AU-6, CA-7, IR-4, SI-4

TABLE 8-12: (cont'd)

	DE.AE-3: Event data are aggregated and correlated from multiple sources and sensors	**ISA 62443-3-3:2013** SR 6.1
		NIST SP 800-53 Rev. 4 AU-6, CA-7, IR-4, IR-5, IR-8, SI-4
	DE.AE-4: Impact of events is determined	**COBIT 5** APO12.06
		NIST SP 800-53 Rev. 4 CP-2, IR-4, RA-3, SI-4
	DE.AE-5: Incident alert thresholds are established	**COBIT 5** APO12.06
		ISA 62443-2-1:2009 4.2.3.10
		NIST SP 800-53 Rev. 4 IR-4, IR-5, IR-8

Detecting anomalies and events is meaningless unless someone notices the detected signals; organizations must therefore implement continuous monitoring in order to detect cyber threats adequately (DE.CM; see table 8-13). This is a critical step because it will allow courts to detect threat signals early and proactively, and work to combat them before there is a substantial breach. Importantly during this step, courts are directed to monitor external service providers who may have access to the court's internal network.

TABLE 8-13:
Framework Core: Security Continuous Monitoring

DETECT (DE)	**Security Continuous Monitoring (DE.CM):** The information system and assets are monitored at discrete intervals to identify cybersecurity events and verify the effectiveness of protective measures.	**DE.CM-1:** The network is monitored to detect potential cybersecurity events	**CCS CSC** 14, 16
			COBIT 5 DSS05.07
			ISA 62443-3-3:2013 SR 6.2
			NIST SP 800-53 Rev. 4 AC-2, AU-12, CA-7, CM-3, SC-5, SC-7, SI-4
		DE.CM-2: The physical environment is monitored to detect potential cybersecurity events	**ISA 62443-2-1:2009** 4.3.3.3.8
			NIST SP 800-53 Rev. 4 CA-7, PE-3, PE-6, PE-20
		DE.CM-3: Personnel activity is monitored to detect potential cybersecurity events	**ISA 62443-3-3:2013** SR 6.2
			ISO/IEC 27001:2013 A.12.4.1
			NIST SP 800-53 Rev. 4 AC-2, AU-12, AU-13, CA-7, CM-10, CM-11

TABLE 8-13: (cont'd)

	DE.CM-4: Malicious code is detected	**CCS CSC** 5
		COBIT 5 DSS05.01
		ISA 62443-2-1:2009 4.3.4.3.8
		ISA 62443-3-3:2013 SR 3.2
		ISO/IEC 27001:2013 A.12.2.1
		NIST SP 800-53 Rev. 4 SI-3
	DE.CM-5: Unauthorized mobile code is detected	**ISA 62443-3-3:2013** SR 2.4
		ISO/IEC 27001:2013 A.12.5.1
		NIST SP 800-53 Rev. 4 SC-18, SI-4. SC-44
	DE.CM-6: External service provider activity is monitored to detect potential cybersecurity events	**COBIT 5** APO07.06
		ISO/IEC 27001:2013 A.14.2.7, A.15.2.1
		NIST SP 800-53 Rev. 4 CA-7, PS-7, SA-4, SA-9, SI-4
	DE.CM-7: Monitoring for unauthorized personnel, connections, devices, and software is performed	**NIST SP 800-53 Rev. 4** AU-12, CA-7, CM-3, CM-8, PE-3, PE-6, PE-20, SI-4
	DE.CM-8: Vulnerability scans are performed	**COBIT 5** BAI03.10
		ISA 62443-2-1:2009 4.2.3.1, 4.2.3.7
		ISO/IEC 27001:2013 A.12.6.1
		NIST SP 800-53 Rev. 4 RA-5

The "detection" step culminates with maintenance of the detection processes (DE.DP; see table 8-14). This means that courts must define employee roles for the detection process in order to ensure accountability. Courts are also to regularly test and improve their detection processes.

TABLE 8-14:
Framework Core: Detection Processes

DETECT (DE)	**Detection Processes (DE.DP):** Detection processes and procedures are maintained and tested to ensure timely and adequate awareness of anomalous events.	**DE.DP-1:** Roles and responsibilities for detection are well defined to ensure accountability	**CCS CSC** 5
			COBIT 5 DSS05.01
			ISA 62443-2-1:2009 4.4.3.1
			ISO/IEC 27001:2013 A.6.1.1
			NIST SP 800-53 Rev. 4 CA-2, CA-7, PM-14
		DE.DP-2: Detection activities comply with all applicable requirements	**ISA 62443-2-1:2009** 4.4.3.2
			ISO/IEC 27001:2013 A.18.1.4
			NIST SP 800-53 Rev. 4 CA-2, CA-7, PM-14, SI-4
		DE.DP-3: Detection processes are tested	**COBIT 5** APO13.02
			ISA 62443-2-1:2009 4.4.3.2
			ISA 62443-3-3:2013 SR 3.3
			ISO/IEC 27001:2013 A.14.2.8
			NIST SP 800-53 Rev. 4 CA-2, CA-7, PE-3, PM-14, SI-3, SI-4
		DE.DP-4: Event detection information is communicated to appropriate parties	**COBIT 5** APO12.06
			ISA 62443-2-1:2009 4.3.4.5.9
			ISA 62443-3-3:2013 SR 6.1
			ISO/IEC 27001:2013 A.16.1.2
			NIST SP 800-53 Rev. 4 AU-6, CA-2, CA-7, RA-5, SI-4
		DE.DP-5: Detection processes are continuously improved	**COBIT 5** APO11.06, DSS04.05
			ISA 62443-2-1:2009 4.4.3.4
			ISO/IEC 27001:2013 A.16.1.6
			NIST SP 800-53 Rev. 4, CA-2, CA-7, PL-2, RA-5, SI-4, PM-14

[D] Respond

The Framework Core then turns to responses, the first segment of which deals with response planning (RS.RP; see table 8-15). It is critical to execute a response to a successful or attempted breach in a timely and efficient manner. Courts may be chaotic places during or in the wake of a breach, but working from a planned response will ensure that the event is handled as efficiently and as properly as possible.

TABLE 8-15:
Framework Core: Response Planning

<table>
<tr><td rowspan="5">RESPOND (RS)</td><td rowspan="5">Response Planning (RS.RP): Response processes and procedures are executed and maintained to ensure timely response to detected cybersecurity events.</td><td rowspan="5">RS.RP-1: Response plan is executed during or after an event</td><td>COBIT 5 BAI01.10</td></tr>
<tr><td>CCS CSC 18</td></tr>
<tr><td>ISA 62443-2-1:2009 4.3.4.5.1</td></tr>
<tr><td>ISO/IEC 27001:2013 A.16.1.5</td></tr>
<tr><td>NIST SP 800-53 REV. 4 CP-2, CP-10, IR-4, IR-8</td></tr>
</table>

We now turn to communications (RS.CO; see table 8-16). This is an important step because the specific ways a court communicates its breach can be of utmost importance. It is important for a court to get appropriate personnel at all levels involved in the process early to ensure the maximum likelihood of executing a proper response to the event.

TABLE 8-16:
Framework Core: Communications

<table>
<tr><td rowspan="11">RESPOND (RS)</td><td rowspan="11">Communications (RS.CO): Response activities are coordinated with internal and external stakeholders, as appropriate, to include external support from law enforcement agencies.</td><td rowspan="3">RS.CO-1: Personnel know their roles and order of operations when a response is needed</td><td>ISA 62443-2-1:2009 4.3.4.5.2, 4.3.4.5.3, 4.3.4.5.4</td></tr>
<tr><td>ISO/IEC 27001:2013 A.6.1.1, A.16.1.1</td></tr>
<tr><td>NIST SP 800-53 Rev. 4 CP-2, CP-3, IR-3, IR-8</td></tr>
<tr><td rowspan="3">RS.CO-2: Events are reported consistent with established criteria</td><td>ISA 62443-2-1:2009 4.3.4.5.5</td></tr>
<tr><td>ISO/IEC 27001:2013 A.6.1.3, A.16.1.2</td></tr>
<tr><td>NIST SP 800-53 Rev. 4 AU-6, IR-6, IR-8</td></tr>
<tr><td rowspan="3">RS.CO-3: Information is shared consistent with response plans</td><td>ISA 62443-2-1:2009 4.3.4.5.2</td></tr>
<tr><td>ISO/IEC 27001:2013 A.16.1.2</td></tr>
<tr><td>NIST SP 800-53 Rev. 4 CA-2, CA-7, CP-2, IR-4, IR-8, PE-6, RA-5, SI-4</td></tr>
<tr><td rowspan="2">RS.CO-4: Coordination with stakeholders occurs consistent with response plans</td><td>ISA 62443-2-1:2009 4.3.4.5.5</td></tr>
<tr><td>NIST SP 800-53 Rev. 4 CP-2, IR-4, IR-8</td></tr>
</table>

TABLE 8-16: (cont'd)

	RS.CO-5: Voluntary information sharing occurs with external stakeholders to achieve broader cybersecurity situational awareness	**NIST SP 800-53 Rev. 4** PM-15, SI-5

The Framework Core then directs organizations to analyze the event (see table 8-17) in order to ensure meaningful recovery activities. Cyberattacks in today's world are an inevitability. The ability to understand and analyze an attack can be invaluable in preventing future attacks. Forensics play a critical role in understanding the attack and preparing for future ones.

TABLE 8-17:
Framework Core: Analysis

RESPOND (RS)	**Analysis (RS.AN):** Analysis is conducted to ensure adequate response and to support recovery activities.	**RS.AN-1:** Notifications from detection systems are investigated	**COBIT 5** DSS02.07
			ISA 62443-2-1:2009 4.3.4.5.6, 4.3.4.5.7, 4.3.4.5.8
			ISA 62443-3-3:2013 SR 6.1
			ISO/IEC 27001:2013 A.12.4.1, A.12.4.3, A.16.1.5
			NIST SP 800-53 Rev. 4 AU-6, CA-7, IR-4, IR-5, PE-6, SI-4
		RS.AN-2: The impact of the incident is understood	**ISA 62443-2-1:2009** 4.3.4.5.6, 4.3.4.5.7, 4.3.4.5.8
			ISO/IEC 27001:2013 A.16.1.6
			NIST SP 800-53 Rev. 4 CP-2, IR-4
		RS.AN-3: Forensics are performed	**ISA 62443-3-3:2013** SR 2.8, SR 2.9, SR 2.10, SR 2.11, SR 2.12, SR 3.9, SR 6.1
			ISO/IEC 27001:2013 A.16.1.7
			NIST SP 800-53 Rev. 4 AU-7, IR-4
		RS.AN-4: Incidents are categorized consistent with response plans	**ISA 62443-2-1:2009** 4.3.4.5.6
			ISO/IEC 27001:2013 A.16.1.4
			NIST SP 800-53 Rev. 4 CP-2, IR-4, IR-5, IR-8

In addition to analyzing the attack, organizations must also contain and mitigate the effects of the attack (RS.MI; see table 8-18). The scope of an attack can be incredibly wide-ranging. In the wake of an event, courts must ensure that they have properly contained the attack and mitigated any harm that may have resulted from it.

TABLE 8-18:
Framework Core: Mitigation

RESPOND (RS)	**Mitigation (RS.MI):** Activities are performed to prevent expansion of an event, mitigate its effects, and eradicate the incident.	**RS.MI-1:** Incidents are contained	**ISA 62443-2-1:2009** 4.3.4.5.6
			ISA 62443-3-3:2013 SR 5.1, SR 5.2, SR 5.4
			ISO/IEC 27001:2013 A.16.1.5
			NIST SP 800-53 Rev. 4 IR-4
		RS.MI-2: Incidents are mitigated	**ISA 62443-2-1:2009** 4.3.4.5.6, 4.3.4.5.10
			ISO/IEC 27001:2013 A.12.2.1, A.16.1.5
			NIST SP 800-53 Rev. 4 IR-4
		RS.MI-3: Newly identified vulnerabilities are mitigated or documented as accepted risks	**ISO/IEC 27001:2013** A.12.6.1
			NIST SP 800-53 Rev. 4 CA-7, RA-3, RA-5

Finally, the "response" section ends with the directive that organizations must improve their response plans (see table 8-19). After an attack, a court may learn a great deal about its own systems as well as the types of threats it may face. This knowledge must be incorporated into future plans, as cyber threats will only become more and more common.

TABLE 8-19:
Framework Core: Improvements

RESPOND (RS)	**Improvements (RS.IM):** Organizational response activities are improved by incorporating lessons learned from current and previous detection and response activities.	**RS.IM-1:** Response plans incorporate lessons learned	**COBIT 5** BAI01.13
			ISA 62443-2-1:2009 4.3.4.5.10, 4.4.3.4
			ISO/IEC 27001:2013 A.16.1.6
			NIST SP 800-53 Rev. 4 CP-2, IR-4, IR-8
		RS.IM-2: Response strategies are updated	**NIST SP 800-53 Rev. 4** CP-2, IR-4, IR-8

[E] Recover

The final tier of the Framework Core addresses recovery from an attack. This process begins with implementing a recovery plan (RC.RP; see table 8-20). In the wake of an attack, it is important to ensure that a court restores and updates its systems and assets. Although a breach can be incredibly harmful to a court, nothing can diminish the importance of moving on from the attack and getting the court back to work.

TABLE 8-20:
Framework Core: Recovery Planning

RECOVER (RC)	**Recovery Planning (RC.RP):** Recovery processes and procedures are executed and maintained to ensure timely restoration of systems or assets affected by cybersecurity events.	**RC.RP-1:** Recovery plan is executed during or after an event	**CCS CSC** 8
			COBIT 5 DSS02.05, DSS03.04
			ISO/IEC 27001:2013 A.16.1.5
			NIST SP 800-53 Rev. 4 CP-10, IR-4, IR-8

Much as a court must update its response plans after an attack, and thereby incorporate what it has learned, it should also update its recovery plans to ensure a better and more efficient recovery in the event of a future attack (see table 8-21). Additionally, it is critical to share such information within a court system so others who are similarly situated may learn from the court's experience.

TABLE 8-21:
Framework Core: Improvements

RECOVER (RC)	**Improvements (RC.IM):** Recovery planning and processes are improved by incorporating lessons learned into future activities.	**RC.IM-1:** Recovery plans incorporate lessons learned	**COBIT 5** BAI05.07
			ISA 62443-2-1 4.4.3.4
			NIST SP 800-53 Rev. 4 CP-2, IR-4, IR-8
		RC.IM-2: Recovery strategies are updated	**COBIT 5** BAI07.08
			NIST SP 800-53 Rev. 4 CP-2, IR-4, IR-8

Finally, the Framework Core concludes with communications (RC.CO; see table 8-22), wherein organizations are to communicate, both internally and externally, in order to maximize reputational repair. It is important for a court to recognize that its public image must be restored, and that confidence in its security must be returned to current and future litigants.

TABLE 8-22:
Framework Core: Communications

RECOVER (RC)	**Communications (RC.CO):** Restoration activities are coordinated with internal and external parties, such as coordinating centers, Internet service providers, owners of attacking systems, victims, other CSIRTs, and vendors.	**RC.CO-1:** Public relations are managed	**COBIT 5** EDM03.02
		RC.CO-2: Reputation after an event is repaired	**COBIT 5** MEA03.02
		RC.CO-3: Recovery activities are communicated to internal stakeholders and executive and management teams	**NIST SP 800-53 Rev. 4** CP-2, IR-4

§ 8.04 ASSESSING CYBERSECURITY RISK MANAGEMENT PRACTICES USING THE FRAMEWORK IMPLEMENTATION TIERS

[A] The Framework Implementation Tiers

A "tier" within the Framework describes the

> . . . degree to which an organization's cybersecurity risk management practices exhibit the characteristics defined in the Framework (e.g., risk and threat aware, repeatable, and adaptive). The Tiers characterize an organization's practices over a range, from Partial (Tier 1) to Adaptive (Tier 4). These Tiers reflect a progression from informal, reactive responses to approaches that are agile and risk-informed. During the Tier selection process, an organization should consider its current risk management practices, threat environment, legal and policy requirements, mission objectives, and organizational constraints.[10]

Progression to higher tiers is encouraged when such a change would reduce cybersecurity risk and be cost effective. Successful implementation of the Framework is based

[10] *See* Framework, *supra* note 9, at 5.

upon achievement of the outcomes described in the organization's target profile or profiles as described in section 8.03 of this chapter, rather than upon a determination of its tier.

[B] The Framework Profiles: Snapshots of an Organization's Cybersecurity Practices

The Framework "profiles" are a mechanism that let an organization signal its overall state of cybersecurity risk management, including how its cybersecurity activities align with operational requirements, risk tolerance, and resources. The profiles support mission requirements and aid in communicating risk within and between organizations. An organization may create a "Current Profile," which is a snapshot of an organization's existing cybersecurity practices, as well as a "Target Profile" that reflects the desired state of its future practices. Organizations may compare these profiles to identify gaps and provide a roadmap for migrating to the target state.

A court can use the Framework as a key part of its systematic process for identifying, assessing, and managing cybersecurity risk. NIST standards do not necessarily have to replace existing processes; a court can use its current process, overlay it onto the Framework to determine gaps in its current cybersecurity risk approach, and develop a roadmap for improvement from there. The Framework is useful at a high level, but NIST Special Publication 800-53, ISO standard 27001, and other recognized cybersecurity standards provide a more detailed set of guidance on various aspects of cybersecurity. By utilizing the Framework as a cybersecurity risk management tool, a court can determine which activities are most important to its operation and litigants, and which resources will maximize the impact of its investment in cybersecurity.

Risk assessments are a fundamental component of a comprehensive cybersecurity program. For courts, some of the relevant considerations for conducting a risk assessment may include the following:[11]

- What are the information technology network boundaries? If there are offices at multiple locations with many devices (laptops, tablets, smartphones, devices from home), there are probably larger risks, so more robust security defenses may be necessary.[12]
- What data does the court store and exchange? Depending on the sensitivity of the data stored at a court, or on particular systems within a court, different degrees of security will be necessary. It is also important to understand what the expectations of internal and external users are with respect to information held by the court.
- Who is inside the network's boundary? If there are contractors with direct access to the court's internal network, there is a greater insider threat than in a system limited to court staff only.

[11] NIST Special Publication (SP) 800-39, *Managing Information Security Risk* (Mar. 2011); NIST SP 800–37, Rev. 1, *Guide for Applying the Risk Management Framework to Federal Information Systems* (Feb. 2010).

[12] *See also* IBM, *supra* note 6.

- What are the security controls? With bigger risks, courts will likely need more layers of more robust security controls.
- How are the risks evolving? As the risks escalate and shift over time, a court's cybersecurity controls must adapt to the changing threat environment. This is why it is crucial not only to be aware that the risks are changing but also to understand as precisely as possible *how* they are changing.

These factors are key examples of what goes into the risk assessments without which there is no way to evaluate the effectiveness of a court's cybersecurity defenses.[13]

[13] David Z. Bodenheimer & Cheryl A. Falvey, *Cybersecurity Standards and Risk Assessments for Law Offices: Weighing the Security Risks and Safeguarding Against Cyber Threats*, https://www.crowell.com/files/Cybersecurity-Standards-and-Risk-Assessments-for-Law-Offices.pdf.

CHAPTER 9

STRUCTURE YOUR COURT TO MAKE IT HACKER-PROOF

Daniel Garrie, Esq., Judge Leo M. Gordon, Greg Kelley, and Bill Spernow

§ 9.01 Internal Network Controls

§ 9.02 Threat Management Versus Risk Management

§ 9.03 Staff—Finding the Right People and Services

§ 9.04 Summary

Previous chapters have focused on perimeter measures that can be taken to keep hackers out of your court's system. Unfortunately, these are imperfect, which means that sometimes hackers can gain access to elements of your computer system. Courts are not helpless if this happens. With strong internal controls, thoughtful threat management, and competent staff, a court can in fact effectively mitigate and eliminate the damage that might result from a hacker penetrating its system.

§ 9.01 INTERNAL NETWORK CONTROLS

Even with the best perimeter controls, the possibility always exists that a hacker will get into your environment. The next step in thwarting the hacker is to have internal controls that make it difficult for the hacker to exfiltrate data. There are methods for protecting your data in the event that an unauthorized person gains access.[1] Consider this: An intruder, once inside, will likely be using a compromised user-account. For example, a user in your court might click on a malicious link that allows a hacker to take control of the user's computer. The user's account will most likely allow this hacker to traverse your network from that computer.[2] A situation like this can be mitigated by restricting which users can access what data.[3]

Restricting users' access to data limits what data a hacker can access and steal when a user account or a computer is compromised.[4] Court personnel typically are judges, law clerks, attorneys, paralegals, case management and administrative staff, and financial professionals as well as those in other departments such as information technology (IT) and human resources. Do those in finance need access to the electronic docket and case management files? Do law clerks and case management staff need access to payroll information? Such examples can go on and on; but IT personnel are typically an exception.

Quite often, IT staff have access to almost anywhere in the environment. They must be able to access various areas to assist the court in carrying out its mission. Furthermore, their access to administrative accounts often gives them access to the entire environment.[5] Best practices for IT staff dealing with network administrative duties are as follows:

---

[1] Margaret Rouse, *Internal Control* [definition], TechTarget, http://searchcompliance.techtarget.com/definition/internal-control.

[2] Christian Cawley, *How Do Trojan Horses Work?*, BrightHub (May 16, 2010), http://www.brighthub.com/computing/smb-security/articles/71376.aspx.

[3] Macky Cruz, *Data Exfiltration in Targeted Attacks*, TrendMicro (Sept. 23, 2013), http://blog.trendmicro.com/trendlabs-security-intelligence/data-exfiltration-in-targeted-attacks/.

[4] *See* Federal Trade Commission (FTC), *Start with Security: A Guide for Business*, https://www.ftc.gov/tips-advice/business-center/guidance/start-security-guide-business ("Not everyone on your staff needs unrestricted access to your network and the information stored on it. Put controls in place to make sure employees have access only on a "need to know" basis. . . . If employees don't have to use personal information as part of their job, there's no need for them to have access to it.").

[5] Warwick Ashford, *One in Four IT Security Staff Abuse Admin Rights, Survey Shows,* Computer Weekly (Dec. 5, 2011), http://www.computerweekly.com/news/2240111956/One-in-four-IT-security-staff-abuse-admin-rights-survey-shows.

- Each IT staff member typically has two accounts: One account is for network administrative work and the other is the IT staff member's day-to-day account. The network administrative account should be used sparingly—only when administrative rights are needed in order to make necessary changes or take necessary actions.[6] Administrative accounts should not be used by IT staff for browsing the Internet, checking email, or doing such daily tasks that are the most likely entry-points for hackers looking to compromise IT accounts. This can decrease the likelihood of an administrative account breach.[7]
- Each IT staff member should have his or her own administrative account.[8] Sharing of administrative accounts can interfere with accountability.[9] If a shared administrative account is compromised, it will be difficult to determine which IT person was responsible for the compromise, and difficult to develop a timeline as to what data may have been stolen.[10]

We have previously discussed intrusion detection systems (IDSs) and firewalls, but the context of the earlier discussion was a court's interaction with the Internet—the external environment. Systems can also be put in place to monitor the opening and accessing of files inside a network.[11] Which computers are accessing the court's payroll, and is that normal? Which employee accounts are accessing certain docket and case-management records, and are those employees even working on those cases? It is important to monitor this data and use it to create a baseline so that abnormal access can be identified.[12]

Firewalls can also be placed inside of a network to protect certain servers and their data from the rest of the court. Typically, an employee would not use a file-server containing docket and case-management files to browse the Internet. Likewise, that server would not be used to access someone's email and open attachments. Limiting those activities on a file-server helps protect that server from being compromised. The other way that our server in question can be compromised is when other workstations in the environment are compromised. The compromised workstations can then be used to attack the file-server. Putting a firewall in place between your file-servers and the workstations

---

[6] *What Is a Network Administrator Account?*, Microsoft, https://technet.microsoft.com/en-us/library/network-admin-account-1.aspx.

[7] For a discussion on what might occur if an administrative account is compromised, *see* Jesper Johansson, *Why You Should Disable the Administrator Account*, Microsoft:TechNet (Jan.-Feb. 2006), https://technet.microsoft.com/en-us/magazine/2006.01.securitywatch.aspx.

[8] David J. Johnson, *The Use and Administration of Shared Accounts,* SANS (2003), https://www.sans.org/reading-room/whitepapers/basics/administration-shared-accounts-1271.

[9] *Id.* ("There is also minimal accountability for shared accounts as users do what they want/need with the accounts but the account really isn't their account.")

[10] *Id.*

[11] Margaret Rouse, *Security Information Management (SIM)* [definition], TechTarget, http://searchsecurity.techtarget.com/definition/security-information-management-SIM.

[12] *Risk Management: Implementation of Baseline Controls*, TechTarget, http://searchsecurity.techtarget.com/tutorial/Risk-management-Implementation-of-baseline-controls.

on your network can limit traffic between those devices.[13] And limiting the traffic limits in turn the types and number of attacks that can take place on a server, helping to protect the server and its contents.[14]

§ 9.02 THREAT MANAGEMENT VERSUS RISK MANAGEMENT

Protecting a court's data starts with understanding its assets, the threats to those assets, how those assets are vulnerable, and the eventual risk to the environment in the event an asset is breached.[15] A court's assets include not only the data it maintains but also the devices that hold, transmit, and protect that data. *Vulnerabilities* are their weaknesses, and they can either be inherent in the technology or due to someone interacting with those assets.[16] *Threats* are the people (hackers) as well as the tools (malware and social engineering) hackers use to attempt to gain access to the assets—usually by exploiting a vulnerability.[17] *Risk* is the likelihood that assets will be exposed combined with the damage done when an asset is exposed.[18]

Practicing threat management is an important element of protecting a court's assets and keeping hackers from getting at your sensitive information. It takes an understanding of the variety of threats out there, from both the technological as well as the human perspective. Identifying threats as soon as they become known is the first—and possibly the most important—step in protecting your environment. By managing threats, a company can mitigate risks.

Threat management allows an organization to respond quickly to evolving threats to its environment. This involves intelligence gathering that allows an organization to spot threats early and before they become a problem. Usually, threat management involves implementation of multiple systems that are dynamically updated based on new threats. Below is a list of threat management systems:

- *Antivirus (AV).* Antivirus applications detect, quarantine, and respond to viruses based on file signatures or behavior patterns. Therefore, AV apps must already have experience with a virus in order to detect it. AV solutions are provided by software vendors who have the advantage of a customer base across multiple geographic regions and sectors. As a result, when one organization detects a new virus, the AV provider can quickly update the rest of its installation base.[19]

---

[13] For an example of a firewall that operates within a network to segment servers and workstations, *see, e.g.*, *Internal Segmentation Firewall (ISFW)*, Fortinet, http://www.fortinet.com/solutions/internal-network-segmentation-firewall.html.

[14] *Id.*

[15] *See, e.g.*, Symantec, Assets, Threats and Vulnerabilities: Discovery and Analysis, https://www.symantec.com/content/en/us/enterprise/media/security_response/whitepapers/Risk_Management.pdf.

[16] *Vulnerability*, Techopedia, https://www.techopedia.com/definition/13484/vulnerability.

[17] *Threat*, Techopedia, https://www.techopedia.com/definition/25263/threat.

[18] *Risk Analysis*, Techopedia, https://www.techopedia.com/definition/16522/risk-analysis.

[19] Margaret Rouse, *Antivirus Software* [definition], TechTarget, http://searchsecurity.techtarget.com/definition/antivirus-software.

- *Anti-spam.* While historically spam was more of a nuisance than anything else, it has evolved into a vehicle for social engineering attempts. Threat management utilizes anti-spam software to block potentially malicious emails that may contain malicious attachments or links to malicious websites. Anti-spam systems can block email servers that are known vectors for spam emails. To do this, they employ sources called real-time blackhole lists (RBLs).[20]
- *Content filtering.* With content filtering, website access is monitored and sites are blocked from being viewed. One of the main uses of content filtering is as an HR tool to prevent employees from viewing websites that may be inappropriate for the work environment (pornography, gambling, or hate sites) or otherwise offensive. Often these types of non-mainstream websites are delivery vehicles for malware.[21]
- *Centralized patch management.* Patch management systems make sure updates are applied in a timely fashion to an environment's computers. Patch management systems can also notify IT when a patch is critical and requires immediate attention.[22]
- *Data loss prevention (DLP).* DLP systems monitor activity on a network, including on workstations and servers, in order to detect when sensitive information is accessed or moved in an unauthorized fashion. DLP systems can change to respond to new methods of data exfiltration such as the currently proliferating private cloud storage sites (Dropbox, Box.net, etc.).[23]
- *Training.* Often the most overlooked method of threat management is employee training. Training employees to spot malicious emails or social engineering attempts can be an effective means of stopping those attacks. When new types of threats emerge, communicating with employees about the threats can help stop them in their tracks. Furthermore, regular reminders of the types of threats out there will keep the topic at the front of each employee's mind. Employing a skeptical staff whose members think twice or inquire about an email before they act on it, though such hesitation can sometimes seem a nuisance, is much better than suffering a successful attack.[24]

The strength of threat management systems lies in pooling resources across multiple sectors and geographic locations.[25] A threat detected at a government agency, for

[20] *Anti-Spam*, Techopedia, https://www.techopedia.com/definition/1629/anti-spam; *RBL—Realtime Blackhole List*, Webopedia, http://www.webopedia.com/TERM/R/RBL.html.

[21] Margaret Rouse, *Content Filtering (Information Filtering)* [definition], TechTarget, http://searchsecurity.techtarget.com/definition/content-filtering.

[22] Margaret Rouse, *Patch Management* [definition], TechTarget, http://searchenterprisedesktop.techtarget.com/definition/patch-management.

[23] *Data Loss Prevention (DLP)* [definition], WhatIs.com, http://whatis.techtarget.com/definition/data-loss-prevention-DLP.

[24] *See, e.g.*, Margaret Rouse, *Security Awareness Training* [definition], TechTarget, http://searchsecurity.techtarget.com/definition/security-awareness-training.

[25] Jacob Williams, *Practical Threat Management and Incident Response for the Small- to Medium-Sized Enterprises*, SANS (June 2014), https://www.sans.org/reading-room/whitepapers/analyst/practical-threat-management-incident-response-small-medium-sized-enterprises-35257.

instance, can result in the implementation of protection-and-prevention techniques by courts hearing challenges to that government agency's decisions. A threat detected at the beginning of the workday in one part of the world can stimulate the release of a patch or update before the workday begins in the United States. Statistics published in an earlier year's Verizon Data Breach Investigations Report have indicated that proper threat management can prevent many breaches by providing a process for updating systems before an attack occurs.[26]

Threats come in a variety of forms. They can be internal or external. They may be human or electronic in nature. A threat can come in an email, from a website, or in someone sitting in front of a computer on the Internet.[27]

The biggest threat to an organization is often internal.[28] Employees are given access to data because they need it to do their work—and frequently their access is unfettered for fear that limitations or controls will impede them. Courts rarely monitor the data employees are accessing and what they are doing with it. Some employees, motivated by greed or disappointment in their job, might abuse their access to court data. Careless or untrained employees can also pose a threat.[29] Maybe such individuals transfer sensitive data to unencrypted USB drives. Or they email sensitive data to an unsecure personal account so they can work from home. Understanding the nature of the employee as a threat is critical to developing policies and processes to safeguard your data.[30] An initial step in the process may be to compartmentalize court data in the first place: This makes it easier to limit employee access to court data only to what each really needs, rather than let all of them have across-the-board access.[31] Next steps may be to limit or even altogether eliminate the use of USB devices.[32] For larger courts with bigger budgets, their understanding of the internal threat may lead them to implement data-loss-prevention technologies that identify, monitor, and scan information in their environment, and that alert the security team to violations of rules set up to control that information.[33]

Another threat comes from social engineering, that is, from the interaction between your employees and the outside world. Social engineering is not a new phenomenon developed with computers. Humans trusting other humans and then falling victim to lies and misdirection is on display in the old story of the Trojan horse. In fact, our use of the

---

[26] *2015 Data Breach Investigations Report*, Verizon Enterprise Solutions, https://msisac.cisecurity.org/whitepaper/documents/1.pdf.

[27] For a more in-depth discussion of the types of cyber threats that a firm may face, see Chapter 3.

[28] Warwick Ashford, *Internal Threat Among Biggest Cyber Security Challenges, Says Former FBI Investigator*, Computer Weekly (June 29, 2015), http://www.computerweekly.com/news/4500248908/Internal-threat-among-biggest-cyber-security-challenges-says-former-FBI-investigator.

[29] Neal O'Farrell, *Employees: Your Best Defense, or Your Greatest Vulnerability*, TechTarget, http://searchsecurity.techtarget.com/tip/Employees-Your-best-defense-or-your-greatest-vulnerability.

[30] *Id.*

[31] *Security Mistakes That Leave You Vulnerable to Compromise #7: Failure to Compartmentalize Your Network*, NetCraftsmen (Sept. 25, 2011), http://www.netcraftsmen.com/security-mistakes-that-leave-you-vulnerable-to-compromise-7-failure-to-compartmentalize-your-network/.

[32] Andy Greenberg, *Why the Security of USB Is Fundamentally Broken*, Wired (July 31, 2014), http://www.wired.com/2014/07/usb-security/.

[33] *Data Loss Prevention (DLP)*, WhatIs.com, http://whatis.techtarget.com/definition/data-loss-prevention-DLP.

word "Trojan" to describe certain types of malware is borrowed from that story. Today social engineering is typically seen in email and telephone communications. Often, social engineering aims to get the target to act on an email that may contain an attachment. When opened, the attachment surreptitiously starts the process of encrypting all data, rendering the data inaccessible and the company a hostage. Or the email contains a link aimed at getting employees to download malicious software or provide credentials in order to "verify" their account. These are but a few of the many forms social engineering can take.

§ 9.03 STAFF—FINDING THE RIGHT PEOPLE AND SERVICES

Courts relying on computers and digital information need a staff to manage that data.[34,35] In small courts, the person in charge of IT unfortunately is often either a young employee who knows more about computers than anyone else at the court or an office administrator without specific training. With today's cybersecurity threats and increased emphasis on protecting data, there are few worse courses a court can take than not having the proper staff.[36]

The old adage "You don't know what you don't know" applies to information technology and cybersecurity in a profound way. Readers might recall the early days of IT when firewall controls were not tight enough; an outside vendor could come in to perform some overflow task that involved scanning the network perimeter. The result would be the embarrassing discovery that the outside vendor was able to read the entire active directory and iterate through all of the user accounts and other objects. Fast-forward a few years: Maybe you can recall speaking to an entity whose computer was being investigated because a former employee of the organization had allegedly stolen information during the last few days of employment. The organization was extremely keen to learn who had opened what files, and when. The organization then described what it did with the computer: With the employee gone, it had turned the computer on and opened nearly every important file on it. So who was the last person to open up these important files and when did they do it? Why, it was the organization itself, after the employee left!

A misconception about computers and IT professionals is that a person in an organization who "knows the most" about computers can handle almost anything. The truth is that the computer industry is filled with specializations the same way the medical and legal industries are.[37] Typically, no one would hire an attorney who specializes in tax law

---

[34] *Every Company Needs to Have a Security Program*, AppliedTrust (2008), https://www.appliedtrust.com/resources/security/every-company-needs-to-have-a-security-program.

[35] *See, e.g.*, Arif Mohamed, *IT Outsourcing for Small Businesses (SMEs)—Essential Guide*, Computer Weekly (July 2009), http://www.computerweekly.com/feature/IT-outsourcing-for-small-businesses-SMEs-Essential-Guide.

[36] Luke Forsyth, *Poor Data Security Can Cause Lasting Damage to Your Enterprise*, The Guardian (Dec. 13, 2012), http://www.theguardian.com/media-network/media-network-blog/2012/dec/13/internet-data-security-enterprise.

[37] Chris Levin, *8 Kinds of IT Professionals: Which One Does Your Company Need?*, AnswerQuest (Aug. 4, 2015), http://answerquest.net/8-kinds-of-it-professionals-which-one-does-your-company-need/.

to obtain advice on labor and employment issues, and no one would seek out a cardiologist to repair a knee gone sideways in a skiing accident. With information technology, there are just as many specialties, including the following:

- **Programmers.** Individuals specializing in programming have intimate knowledge of one or more programming languages. These individuals understand the methods and processes undertaken to model a product, design the interface (with inputs and outputs), and program the application in the most efficient way.[38] And in reality, the programming specialty can be further broken down by knowledge of different programming languages.
- **Desktop Support.** Desktop support personnel understand the standard computer setup as well as the programs being run at the court. Their knowledge and experience helps them determine the best ways to support and fix computers as well as how to research problems in a timely manner.[39]
- **Database Administrator.** Larger courts relying on applications that interface with Oracle, SQL Server, or another database application need individuals who specialize in databases. These individuals can model an environment and convert it into a series of tables, fields, and queries that store information about the environment. Database administrators understand how to maximize the efficiency of a database so that it can store and serve up large amounts of data in an acceptable time frame.[40]
- **Network administrator.** These individuals have responsibilities that may include managing the switches, routers, and hubs that form the physical backbone of a court's network. They may also have responsibilities related to adding, removing, and otherwise managing user-accounts. Network administrators may also deal with a court's email system, although that, too, can be a specialty in and of itself.[41]
- **Information security.** Information security specialists have the responsibility of ensuring that a court's digital information is protected. Their realm of influence includes setting security policies (such as password policies that are implemented by others), configuring firewalls, and monitoring a court's network for signs of intrusion. Depending on the size of the team and its makeup, information security specialists may be involved not only in preventing attacks but also, when an attack has occurred, in investigating it.[42]

The preceding descriptions are merely a sampling of the numerous specialties within the information technology field. Even these may indeed be too general for some people's tastes. But the point was to show that it takes the right people with the right skills

[38] *Id.*
[39] *Id.*
[40] *Id.*
[41] *Id.*
[42] *Id.*

to handle the various aspects of information technology, especially information security.[43]

Not every court can afford to hire multiple IT staff members. But when filling the positions you have, it is important to hire people with the proper mindset when it comes to security. Policies, systems, applications, etc. all should be designed with security in mind from the beginning.[44] Many courts choose to share data with litigants and law firms.[45] The first question the designers of the portal should ask should be: What type of information will be shared? The second is: How will that information be protected?[46] It is the responsibility of the IT security department to raise those questions.

The right IT security professionals will understand that they are underequipped the minute they begin.[47] IT security is a lot like being an offensive lineman on a football team. Think about the last game you watched: Do you remember the 50 plays in which the offensive tackle successfully blocked the defensive lineman, or do you remember that one play where the defensive lineman got through and sacked the quarterback? Managing IT security is very similar in that success means protecting the environment against any and all attacks, whereas the successful hacker need only get through once.[48] The right IT security professional understands this concept and will use the resources at hand to practice threat management as discussed in the previous section.

IT security professionals also understand that they are a team of one; or, in very large courts, one of a team of multiple people.[49] And they also know that they face an opponent split into teams of hundreds or even thousands or more.[50] The hacker world works tirelessly to exploit the latest vulnerabilities and find new ones.[51] Hackers also share a good deal of information.[52] When we add state-sponsored hacking into this mix,

---

[43] David Mortman, *Best Practices for Choosing an Information Security Team New Hire*, TechTarget, http://searchsecurity.techtarget.com/answer/Best-practices-for-choosing-an-information-security-team-new-hire.

[44] *See, e.g., Information Security Policy—A Development Guide for Large and Small Companies*, SANS (2007), https://www.sans.org/reading-room/whitepapers/policyissues/information-security-policy-development-guide-large-small-companies-1331.

[45] For an example of an organization that provides secure client portals, see Joanna Slusarz, *How to Securely Share Documents with Clients*, Laserfiche, https://www.laserfiche.com/ecmblog/how-to-securely-share-documents-with-clients/.

[46] Steve Barnes, *Three Basics of Secure Client Portal Design*, Coretech Revolution (June 28, 2012), http://www.coretechrevolution.com/latest-news/139-three-basics-of-secure-client-portal-design.

[47] Gil Press, *6 Observations About Cybersecurity Based on Two New Surveys*, Forbes:Tech (Aug. 12, 2015), http://www.forbes.com/sites/gilpress/2015/08/12/6-observations-about-cybersecurity-based-on-two-new-surveys/#7df04c3d552c.

[48] Chris Triolo, *Hackers Only Need to Get It Right Once, We Need to Get It Right Every Time*, SCMagazine (July 24, 2015), http://www.scmagazine.com/hackers-only-need-to-get-it-right-once-we-need-to-get-it-right-every-time/article/362462/.

[49] Tom Scholtz & Rob McMillan, *Tips and Guidelines for Sizing Your Information Security Organization*, Gartner (Aug. 19, 2015), https://www.gartner.com/doc/2718319/tips-guidelines-sizing-information-security.

[50] Triolo, *supra* note 49.

[51] *Id.*

[52] Tom Groenfeldt, *Hackers Collaborate, Now White Hats Can Share Cyber Crime Info*, Forbes:Tech (Nov. 4, 2013), http://www.forbes.com/sites/tomgroenfeldt/2013/11/04/hackers-collaborate-now-white-hats-can-share-cyber-crime-info/#421a5d3d17a1 ("The bad guys use social media to communicate and share information but the good guys don't do that.").

we realize that hackers have not only more people and more time but also more money and better computing resources.

Good IT security professionals spend time researching and staying up-to-date on the latest security and hacking trends.[53] Be it reading articles and blogs or attending conferences and formal trainings, many avenues are available for continuous learning suited to people with different learning styles on different budgets.[54] It is critical that court leadership as well as everyone else down through the organization take seriously and support IT security.[55]

§ 9.04 SUMMARY

Every court with a computer network is potentially threatened. While hackers specifically target some organizations, most organizations become victims because they took no, or only very minimal, steps to avoid being hacked.[56] It is all too common for an organization's perimeter defenses to be breached; but strong internal controls as well competent staff can be instrumental in mitigating or avoiding harm when a breach does occur. Courts must implement internal controls to protect their data in the event that a system is compromised. Practicing threat management—as opposed to risk management—is a way to create a flexible IT environment that can adapt its protection schemes whenever a novel type of attack comes to light. Threat management also allows for users to be notified when new attacks take place. Finally, the proper staff—be it internal or outsourced—will help put in place the processes discussed in this chapter. Proper security requires a lot of attention and a lot of work; but every court should implement some if not all of these security measures in order to protect its sensitive data. The consequences of not doing may be exponentially more damaging, expensive, and time-consuming than the investment in security.

---

[53] Ondrej Krehel, *Getting Your Information Security Team Right*, CSO (Oct. 14, 2015), http://www.csoonline.com/article/2991282/infosec-staffing/getting-your-information-security-team-right.html.

[54] For a list of some of the places where information security professionals can get this information, see *Top 100+ Cyber Security Blogs & Infosec Resources,* DDOS Protection Services (2016), http://ddosattackprotection.org/blog/cyber-security-blogs/.

[55] AppliedTrust, *supra* note 34.

[56] John Pullen, *How to Protect Your Small Business Against a Cyber Attack*, Entrepreneur (Feb. 27, 2013), https://www.entrepreneur.com/article/225468 ("According to a Verizon study of data breaches in 2011, more than 80 percent of victims were targets of opportunity—which means they did not protect their Wi-Fi systems with passwords and otherwise had poor security, if any at all.").

INDEX

A

Adware, 1.01
Anti-spam, threat management and, 9.02
Anti-virus, threat management and, 9.02
Asymmetric cryptography, 5.01[B], 5.02, 5.04
Asymmetric encryption, 5.02
Attacks, frequency of, 7.02

B

BitLocker, 4.06
Botnet, 3.04[L]
Bots, cyber threats and, 3.04[L]
Bring your own device (BYOD), 4.02
Browser security, cyber threats and, 3.04[K]
Bypassing of security controls, cyber threats and, 3.04[E]

C

Certificate authority (CA), 5.05[A]
Commandments, cybersecurity and, 2.01–2.10
  "Crown Jewels," identify and protect, 2.04
  cyber hygiene, developing and practicing strong, 2.02
  global communications, creating and developing, 2.06
  government relationships, maintaining, 2.10
  incident response plan, practicing and testing, 2.05, 2.07
  messaging framework, creating and developing, 2.06
  privacy and cybersecurity expertise, engaging, 2.09
  robust cyber threat monitoring and sharing team, developing, 2.08
  vendor's networks, securing, 2.03
Courts and courts system
  cybersecurity and, 1.01
  cyber threats and, 7.03
  frequency of attacks, 7.02
  hackers and, 7.01
"Crown Jewels," identify and protect, 2.04
Cryptanalysis, 5.01[B]
Cryptography, 5.06[B]
  algorithms, 5.01[B]
  asymmetric, 5.01[B], 5.02
  considerations, 5.06
    jurisdictional law, 5.06[B]
    vendor selection, 5.06[A]
  data disclosure, 5.01[B]
  data encryption, 5.01[B]
  data in storage, 5.01[B]
  data in transit, 5.01[B]
  data modification, 5.01[B]
  entity masquerading, 5.01[B]
  importance of, 5.01[A]
  introduction, 5.01
  key management, 5.01[B], 5.05
    key backup and recovery, 5.05[D]
    key distribution, 5.05[B]
    key expiration, 5.05[F]
    key generation, 5.05[A]
    key revocation, 5.05[E]
    key storage, 5.05[C]
    key termination, 5.05[G]
    secret keys, 5.01[B]
  message authentication, 5.01[B], 5.03
  protocols, 5.01[B]
  public key, 5.01[B]
  symmetric, 5.01[B], 5.02
  vs. encryption, 5.01[B]
Cyberattacks
  frequency of, 7.02
  types of, 1.01
Cyber hygiene, developing and practicing strong, 2.02
Cybersecurity
  commandments of, 2.01–2.10
    "Crown Jewels," identify and protect, 2.04
    cyber hygiene, developing and practicing strong, 2.02
    global communications, creating and developing, 2.06
    government relationships, maintaining, 2.10
    incident response plan, practicing and testing, 2.05, 2.07
    messaging framework, creating and developing, 2.06

Cybersecurity (*cont'd*)
commandments of (*cont'd*)
privacy and cybersecurity expertise, engaging, 2.09
robust cyber threat monitoring and sharing team, developing, 2.08
vendor's networks, securing, 2.03
courts and courts system, 1.01
court vulnerability to, 1.01
critical infrastructure, framework for
assessing cybersecurity risk management practices, 8.04
cybersecurity program, framework core, 8.03
introduction, 8.01
NIST framework, 8.02
defined, 1.01
risk management practices, 8.04
risk management program, 8.03[C]
detection, 8.03[C]
identification, 8.03[A]
protection, 8.03[B]
recovery, 8.03[E]
response, 8.03[D]
Cybersecurity program, framework core, 8.03
Cyber threats, survey of, 3.01–3.04
court systems and, 3.03
types of threats faced by, 7.02
introduction, 3.01
range of specific threats, 3.04[A]–3.04[P]
Bots and, 3.04[L]
browser security, 3.04[K]
bypassing of security controls, 3.04[E]
denial-of-service attacks, 3.04[H]
employee criminality, 3.04[B]
group phishing, 3.04[I]
insider/privilege-abuse hostilities, 3.04[D]
network port probes, 3.04[F]
social engineering, 3.04[C]
spear phishing, 3.04[J]
spyware, 3.04[P]
theft or loss of a device, 3.04[A]
Trojan horses, 3.04[N]
unpatched software vulnerabilities, 3.04[G]
viruses/worms, 3.04[M]
website exploits, 3.04[K]
zero-day exploits, 3.04[O]
risk-based approach, 3.02

D

Data availability, ISO Standard 27001, 6.02[A][3]
Database administrator, 9.03
Data confidentiality, ISO Standard 27001, 6.02[A][1]
Data disclosure, cryptography, 5.01[B]
Data encryption, 5.01[B]
Data in storage, cryptography, 5.01[B]
Data integrity, 5.01[B], 5.04
ISO Standard 27001, 6.02[A][2]
Data in transit, cryptography, 5.01[B]
Data loss prevention, threat management and, 9.02
Data modification, cryptography, 5.01[B]
Decryption, 5.02
Demilitarized zone (DMZ), 4.05
Denial-of-Service attack (DOS attack), 3.04[J]
cyber threats and, 3.04[H]
Desktop support, 9.03
Dictionary attack, 4.02
Digital signature, 5.04
Digital Signature Guideline (DSG), 5.01[B]

E

Electronic signature, 5.01[B]
Employee criminality, cyber threats and, 3.04[B]
Encryption, 4.06, 5.02
vs. cryptography, 5.01[B]
Entity masquerading, cryptography, 5.01[B]

F

Firewalls, 4.03
Forward-facing servers, 4.05
Ftps, 4.06

G

Global communications, creating and developing, 2.06
Government relationships, maintaining, 2.10
Group phishing, cyber threats and, 3.04[I]

H

Hackers
courts and courts system, 7.01
encryption and, 4.06
firewalls and, 4.03
password management and, 4.02
patch management and, 4.04

perimeter security controls and, 4.05
up-to-date software and, 4.04
Hacking tools, 3.03
Https, 4.06

I

Incident response plan, practicing and testing, 2.05, 2.07
Information security, 9.03
Information security management system (ISMS), 6.02[C], 6.03[A], 6.03[B]
Information sharing, defending against threats and, 7.01–7.04
Information sharing and analysis center (ISAC), 7.03
Insider/privilege-abuse hostilities, cyber threats and, 3.04[D]
Internal network controls, 9.01
Internet of Things ("IoT"), 3.02
Intrusion detection systems (IDS), 4.05, 9.01
ISO Standard 27001
ensuring compliance, 6.02[D]
establishing security objectives, 6.02[A]
data availability, 6.02[A][3]
data confidentiality, 6.02[A][1]
data integrity, 6.02[A][2]
identifying security needs, 6.02[B]
implementing a security program, 6.02[C]
statement of applicability, 6.03[C]
ISO standards
introduction, 6.01
ISO Standard 27001. *See* ISO Standard 27001
overview of, 6.01[A]
scope and certification, 6.03
auditing an organization's compliance, 6.03[A]
ISMS, scope of, 6.03[B]

K

Key backup and recovery, 5.05[D]
Key distribution, 5.05[B]
Key establishment, 5.05[B]
Key expiration, 5.05[F]
Key generation, 5.05[A]
Key management, cryptography
key backup and recovery, 5.05[D]
key distribution, 5.05[B]
key expiration, 5.05[F]
key generation, 5.05[A]
key revocation, 5.05[E]
key storage, 5.05[C]
key termination, 5.05[G]
lifecycle, 5.05[A]
Key revocation, 5.05[E]
Key storage, 5.05[C]
Key termination, 5.05[G]

L

Legal Services Information Sharing and Analysts Organization (LS-ISAO), 7.04

M

Message authentication, 5.01[B], 5.03
Messaging framework, creating and developing, 2.06

N

Network administrator, 9.03
Network port probes, cyber threats and, 3.04[F]
NIST framework, 8.02
Nonrepudiation, 5.03, 5.04

P

Password management, 4.02
Password munging, 4.02
Patch management
hackers and, 4.04
threat management and, 9.02
"Patch Tuesday," 3.04[G]
Perimeter security controls, 4.05
Phishing, 1.01, 3.04[I]
Port, 3.04[F]
Privacy and cybersecurity expertise, engaging, 2.09
Programmers, 9.03
Public key cryptography, 5.01[B]
Public key infrastructure (PKI), 5.05[A]

R

Ransomware, 1.01
Realtime blackhole lists (RBLs), 9.02
Risk management practices, assessing cybersecurity, 8.04

Risk management program, cybersecurity
detection, 8.03[C]
identification, 8.03[A]
protection, 8.03[B]
recovery, 8.03[E]
response, 8.03[D]
Risk management *vs.* threat management, 9.02
Robust cyber threat monitoring and sharing team, developing, 2.08

S

Secret keys, 5.01[B]
Secure Sockets Layer (SSL), 4.06
Social engineering
cyber threats and, 3.04[C]
defined, 3.04[C]
Software vulnerabilities, 3.04[G]
Spear phishing, cyber threats and, 3.04[J]
Spyware, cyber threats and, 3.04[P]
Staffs
network administrative duties of, 9.01
selection of, 9.03
Statement of applicability, ISO Standard 27001, 6.03[C]
Symmetric cryptography, 5.01[B], 5.02
Symmetric encryption, 5.02
Symmetric keys, 5.01[B]

T

Theft or loss of a device, cyber threats and, 3.04[A]
Threat management
anti-spam, 9.02
anti-virus, 9.02
centralized patch management, 9.02
content filtering, 9.02
data loss prevention, 9.02
training, 9.02
vs. risk management, 9.02
Trojan horses, cyber threats and, 3.04[N]
Trusted Platform Module (TPM) chip, 4.06
Trusted root certificates, 4.06

U

Uniform Electronic Transactions Act (UETA), 5.01[B]
Unpatched software vulnerabilities, cyber threats and, 3.04[G]
Up-to-date software, 4.04

V

Vendor's networks, securing, 2.03
Viruses/worms, cyber threats and, 3.04[M]
Vulnerabilities, description of, 9.02

W

Website exploits, cyber threats and, 3.04[K]

Z

Zero-day exploits, cyber threats and, 3.04[O]

www.ingramcontent.com/pod-product-compliance
Lightning Source LLC
LaVergne TN
LVHW082341200926
848481LV00012B/3417

* 9 7 8 1 5 4 3 8 0 9 7 5 6 *